GLOW
GETTER

SHANI JAY

I believe in you.

Disclaimer: The methods described within this publication are the author's personal thoughts. The advice and strategies found within may not be suitable for every situation. This work is sold with the understanding that neither the author nor the publisher are held responsible for the results accrued from the advice in this book. This book is not intended to be a substitute for professional medical advice. The reader should consult with their doctor in any matters relating to his/her health.

A catalogue record for this book is available from the British Library.

Connect with Shani: www.shanijay.com

ISBN-13: 978-1-9997674-1-9

For all the women wanting
to step into their new story,
but needing someone
to show them the way...

BEFORE YOU GET STARTED...

Glow Getter is split into 11 chapters, each of which build upon the other, and represent the next step on the way to transforming your life—so please don't skip ahead even if you're tempted to!

Each chapter in this book outlines a different set of challenges you'll have to conquer along your journey, coupled with some of my own personal life lessons, and the powerful wisdom of some incredible women who have inspired me along the way. At the end of each chapter, there is a Glow Guide—a mini workbook and journaling space for you to reflect on what you've learned in that chapter, and start putting those teachings into practice in your own life! You can complete these within the book, or in a gorgeous notebook—the choice is entirely yours.

I've also created a free master **Glow Guide workbook**, which contains all of the mini Glow Guides from this book, plus lots of extra surprises! Head to **shanijay.com/glowguide** to download it right now before you dive in to the book.

#GLOWGETTERTRIBE

CONTENTS

Hey, Glow Getter!

HEY, GLOW GETTER!

Glow Getter

(noun)

An inspirational woman who strives to achieve all her goals in life, lighting up the world with her inner glow.

Have you ever noticed those women who endlessly glow with love and light, from the inside out? Their passion and energy illuminate the world, and you find yourself wondering, *"What's her secret?"* You know deep down there's no reason why you shouldn't be living a fulfilling, beautiful, kick-ass life of your own—but you have no idea how or where to begin.

While making the decision to change your life is easy, actually following through with it, making those changes, and sticking to them? That's damn hard work. I should know, I've been there. Like all things in this world, it's *so* much easier said than done.

You might have no idea where to begin, your friends and family might not be as supportive of your transformation journey as you'd like them to be, you might lose motivation along the way, and the truth is you might even *fail* and fall flat on your face (don't worry—it happens to the best of us).

Wouldn't it be much easier if you enlisted some help along the way?

Maybe you want to lose weight, start eating cleaner and living a healthier lifestyle; maybe you want to start your own business and eventually quit your soul-sucking nine-to-five; or maybe you're finally done with crummy relationships and you want to attract the partner of your dreams? Perhaps even all of the above!

Regardless of why you're on this journey to transform yourself and your life, you need someone there to guide you along the way and spur you on during the toughest moments when you're most likely to lose hope and quit. Because I don't want that for you—I want to give you the best possible chance at flipping your current life around and becoming your best self. Enter, *Glow Getter*.

In this book, I'm going to share the many struggles and obstacles you'll face along the way to transforming your life and provide strategies and tips on how to overcome these challenges, as well as how to change and realign your daily habits in order to give you the best chance at success. Each chapter will outline a different obstacle, with solutions on how to push your way through, and a fun guided exercise at the end for you to complete to help you on your way.

Glow Getter is for any woman who wants to transform her life or is in the process of already making some big changes, but feels overwhelmed by the gravity of the task and needs a helping hand to guide and reassure her along the way. If you know you're not living your best life and you don't feel that gorgeous glow, this book was written for you.

What most of you don't know about me is that back in January 2016, I was working my fifth year in the fashion industry (trust me, it sounds *way* more glamorous than it really is), a career path I decided on at the ripe old age of 17. Fast forward through university and my first few jobs, and you will find me slaving away in a nine-to-five which increasingly began to feel incredibly unfulfilling, like I was trapped in an invisible kind of prison of my own making. I was going nowhere fast. One thing was for certain—

I could not live out the rest of my life this way. I knew something had to change, and change quick.

During this time, I began to pick writing back up as a hobby. I started by submitting my work to various online platforms (for free at first), waking up between 5 and 6 a.m. before work to write, then getting home to start writing again. This became my life for the best part of 10 months, and I quickly realised that writing was what truly made me happy. Even better, I'd be able to work remotely, set my own schedule, and be my own boss—something which I've always craved.

I made the decision in the spring of 2016 to quit my job by the end of the year and pave my own sparkly pink path. It's now August 2017 as I write this and so far my work has been published on numerous platforms including *The Huffington Post, Teen Vogue,* and *Thought Catalog.* I run my own content creation business which allows me to work anywhere in the world AND I became a bestselling author. Oh, and I also managed to *finally* step off the loser train after hanging around for 10 years at A-hole central, meet an awesome guy, and fall in love too!

Not bad for a year's work, right?

But no part of this journey was easy. It was painful, there were many tears along the way, and I'm still figuring things out as I go. Over the past year, I've become the woman I always dreamed of being, so believe me when I tell you it's possible for you too. The only thing that separates us right now is that I decided to be her.

Stick with *Glow Getter* and you'll see the only person truly standing in the way of your dream life is *you*. This book is packed with helpful tips and tricks that have worked for countless successful women already, including me. They will work for you too—all you have to do is pay attention, do the work, and be 100% serious about transforming your life.

I'm going to share with you every part of my journey in going from downright clueless to dialled in. These strategies are an expansion on many of the same ones I share with all of the wonderful women who have joined the Glow Getter Tribe—a female, self-love, and kindness movement I created in 2016.

I promise if you follow the 11 chapters in this book and put them into practice, you will notice how you begin to blossom into the beautiful flower that has been patiently waiting to bloom all this time. You'll have a totally new outlook and mindset, you'll feel more positive and energised, and you'll possess the tools necessary to make all of the changes you desire in order to become a happy, unstoppable woman who glows from the inside out.

How long are you going to carry on waiting to change your life?

How many more women are you going to witness taking the journey to their higher self while you quietly watch from the sidelines?

Don't waste the rest of your life feeling miserable, unfulfilled, and lost.

Stand up today and wholeheartedly commit to your journey in becoming your best self.

Trust me when I say I *know* what it's like to feel like you're living a half-life. I know what it's like to know deep down that you're meant for something more than *this*. And I know what it takes to get yourself from where you are right now to the woman you want to be because I've lived it.

Glow Getter is arranged into easy-to-manage chapters, each one outlining challenges and offering valuable insight into solutions, along with Glow Guides for you to implement right away. All you have to do is keep showing up and reading.

So you've decided you want to transform your life and become the woman you've always dreamed of being? Well, what are you waiting for?

Becoming the woman you want to be is as simple as deciding right now that you're going to *be* her. Pour yourself a delicious drink in the prettiest glass you can find, get comfy, and let's do this, glow getter!

Your best self awaits you inside.

All my love,

Shani x

"The woman you're becoming
will cost you people,
relationships, spaces, and
material things along the way.

Choose her over everything."

— Anon.

FIND YOUR WHY AND
NEVER LET IT GO

"Where you find purpose
Is where you find happiness
And where you find happiness
Is where you find Truth
And when you find Truth
Truth will set you free."

— Suzy Kassem

It's time to step into the beautiful new life you dream of creating—no more excuses, no more waiting until tomorrow. All we have is today, right now, in this moment. Any kind of change can seem overwhelming from the get-go, so we're going to break it down and begin from day one. The hardest part can be getting started, but only if you're not clear on why you really want to turn your life around. So it's time we unlocked your *why*.

Why do you want to transform your life?

Every *what* needs a *why*.

Before we dive into making changes, it's vital you get clear on your **why**. Why do you really want to change? Maybe you want to lose weight so you can start living a healthier, more active lifestyle. Maybe you want to switch careers so you can finally wake up on Monday mornings and look forward to the day ahead. Or maybe you want to focus solely on transforming your inner mindset and attitude so that you can be a better partner or parent to your kids. It might even be a combination of a few different things that all intertwine.

What all of these why's have in common is they centre on you having reached your absolute limits with what your life looks like today. You've finally had enough of living a half, mediocre life. You know this is far from the best you can be. You want more and expect better from yourself because you're aware of the true power you possess within your soul.

Look around you, and you can't help but notice other women living happier, richer, and more vibrant lives than the one you're living. They're out there whipping their dreams up into reality and you wonder, what's their *secret*? How do they do it? Why can't I live the life of my dreams too?

The truth is you absolutely **can**. It is possible for us all.

Deep down I *know* you deserve a beautiful life you're crazy in love with. You deserve to have rainbow confetti piñatas exploding in your skies. You deserve to be the unstoppable woman you know you can be. And deep down, you know it too.

So first things first, get clear on your **why**. It doesn't matter what it is as long as it holds enough weight within your heart. Does it motivate you enough? Does it light your soul on fire with pure passion and determination? Is it going to be enough to get you out of bed at 5 a.m. every morning to work on your side hustle or stop you binge-watching your favourite box sets on Netflix? Is your why going to be enough to keep you moving forward when nothing seems to be going your way and all you can think about is giving up?

Find your why, place it in your heart, and never let it go. You're going to need to call upon it throughout your transformation journey.

Why *now*? What has changed?

Why is *today* different from all your other yesterdays?

Why have you decided to pick up this book *today* of all days and change your life? What was wrong with last week? What about last month? What about last year or the year before that one?

Why does your transformation feel so much more urgent to you now than ever before?

Perhaps you feel that ever so slowly you're running out of time. You keep putting things off—*I'll start tomorrow*, or *I'll start next week*—and before you know it, next week becomes never. Maybe you woke up this morning and something ignited within you. You're not quite sure what it was, but something told you it's now or never. Something called you to open this book and this time you felt compelled to listen. Maybe you feel like your life is quickly passing you by, the weeks and months stripped bare of joy, fulfillment, and passion—emotions you vaguely remember from long ago, but somehow, without you noticing, they gradually faded away until all you were left with was a dull, shell-like existence.

The truth is it's incredibly hard to transform your life on your own, without any kind of outside help or road map to take you to where you want to go. That's why the number of life coaches, personal trainers, and self-help books have skyrocketed in the past decade. More and more people are wanting to reach their higher selves and are enlisting the help of experts to get there as quickly as possible.

You might've already tried to turn over a new leaf in the past but fell short. A New Year's resolution that you lost willpower for by the time March came around. A total revamp of your life that was simply too overwhelming to stick with. Or something unexpected happened along the way, totally threw you off course, and you never managed to navigate your way back.

But what will be different about **today**?

All that truly needs to be different is *you*.

You have to want it this time, and I mean you have to want it desperately. You have to want to transform your life as much as you want to *breathe*. You have to get into the headspace where you are committing wholly to this journey and at no point will you be getting off until you reach your destination. Don't be involved, be *committed*. There will be bumps, U-turns, and potentially some crashes along the way, but you can't let any of those blips stop you from continuing to pave your way forward against the current.

If you want to become the best woman you know you can be, you're going to have to tap into a place deep down within and promise to give it your all. Not 75%, not when you find the time for it, but **everything you've got**.

A true commitment to personal change requires three vital elements:

1. Vision - Being able to clearly visualise what you want and where you hope to go. You don't have to have to know *exactly* where you'll be or what you'll be doing in 10 years' time, but it's important to gain clarity on a couple of key areas where you know you'd like to make big changes.

2. Promise - You have to promise to show up for yourself every single day, no matter what's happening or how exhausted you might be. You must promise yourself that you'll give it your all and won't stop until you reach your goal.

3. Energy - Most importantly, you have to be prepared to put it in the work. Will it be easy? *Hell* no! But will it be worth it? Absofrickin-lutely. Remember, nothing will change unless *you* do.

Right now, make a promise to yourself of commitment to your new journey.

Absolutely nothing can stop me from realising my dreams.
I am 100% willing to show up and do my absolute best at all times.
I dare to put my mind, emotions, and actions to work for what I want most in my life.

Write your own promise below:

Dream BIG

So many of us are terrified to dream big—I used to be too. We worry what other people might say, we fear failure, and we get too comfortable with our current lives even if it's making us miserable. We convince ourselves that we're not worthy of success, abundance, or true happiness—that's reserved only for the celebs and the royalty of this world. And we allow ourselves to become so worked up inside with all these negative thoughts coursing through our minds that we decide it's better to not even *try*—how heartbreaking is that?

The sooner you acknowledge what it is that you desire and realise you don't need to feel guilty, embarrassed, or ashamed for wanting it—and that the fear of failure and the unknown are mostly irrational fears we create in our own minds—the sooner you can embark on this incredible journey of transformation and move closer to your deepest dreams and desires.

Being a writer, I read a *lot*, and my all-time favourite book is *The Alchemist* by Paulo Coelho. The book centres around this beautifully poetic idea that once your heart decides that it wants something, all of the universe will conspire to help you achieve it. Of course, you have to show up and put in the work, but as soon as you do, the universe will start moving to meet you halfway. The truth is the universe *wants* you to live your biggest and boldest life, but you've gotta want it too!

So today, I invite you to think BIGGER than you ever have done.

What is it that you desire most in your life right now? Maybe you want to be a more confident and strong-minded woman who is head over heels in love with her life and doesn't base her worth on opinions of others. Maybe you want to find your way to a career that's both exciting and fulfilling and offers you freedom. Perhaps you're a little lost and not quite sure want you truly want—all you know is life right now is making you far from happy.

Ask yourself, what is it that your heart is set on? What does your mind, body, and soul crave the most in this moment? If you were living your dream life today, what would it look like?

Like I said, don't worry about having all the finer details mapped out, like the street you'll be living on, how many dogs you'll have, or the name of your husband! The truth is it's incredibly hard for any of us to imagine where we'll be in *one* year, let alone the next five or ten. We can push our lives in a certain direction as much as we want, but we can't predict the many surprises life will gift us along the way.

So take a few minutes right now to close your eyes and ponder what a day in your dream life looks like. And remember, nothing is too big or too crazy. The only thing that sets you apart from those women you aspire to be like is your *mind*. Everything is possible, as long as you can visualise it.

When I think about my perfect day, it involves me waking up in a beautiful cocoon-like bed that simulates the feeling of sleeping on clouds. I'll get up, make myself a steaming cup of refreshing green tea, and head to my writing space. My gorgeous white desk is a fountain of inspiration and looks out onto a beautiful garden of pink peonies that I've planted and nurtured myself. I'll spend these early hours journaling and working on my latest book, creating something from nothing, and feeling incredibly grateful that I've created a life where I'm able to do meaningful work that touches other people's hearts. After a couple hours, I'll begin cooking myself a sumptuous breakfast from scratch. In between writing and working on my business the rest of the day, I'll head out for a swim to relax my whole body and mind, melting away any tension or stress lurking. I'm able to book a flight and jet off to an exotic location at short notice and take my writing with me. I have the luxury of working from home and spending precious time with my loved ones. My life is fulfilling, abundant, and inspiring all at once.

I've already managed to turn many of these dreams into a reality, simply by visualising what I want most and believing that it's within my reach—and you can do it too! *Anything* is possible as long as you believe it to be. Believing is half the battle. I believe in you, glow getter; it's about time you did too! You are so incredibly special if only you could see it. Quit thinking you're not worthy of the good life—you're just as worthy as anybody else.

That being said, you might've read similar books to this or stumbled on articles or quotes that speak along the same lines. You might've been sold the idea that if you visualise what you want enough, it will magically appear in your life. And hey, I like to cover things in pink glitter and sparkles as much as the next girl, but this is far from the reality and I'm not gonna lie to you because you deserve the truth.

Visualisation and dreaming are fab, but they mean nothing if you're not prepared to work hard and make some dramatic, often painful, changes. Everything is yours for the taking, if you're prepared to do what it takes. Wishing and hoping can only take you so far—*doing* will take you the rest of the way on your journey.

You're going to have to make sacrifices you don't want to make, you're going to have to put your long-term happiness ahead of short-term pleasure, and you're going to have moments when you feel like giving up and going back to your old ways. This journey will be uncomfortable and possibly the hardest thing you've ever done in your life, but I promise it will also be the **best** thing you ever decide to do.

Make yourself proud

Cast your mind back for a moment to when you were just a little girl. A little girl who was still innocent and brave enough to believe she could be anything and everything she could possibly dream of in her wildest imagination. The whole world was at your feet and the stars above within reach. The younger you probably had far higher hopes and expectations for herself than the you today. When did you decide to let those go? When did you decide to start settling for okay instead of extraordinary?

Think of all the things you said you'd accomplish and all of the great adventures you looked forward to in your future. Remember how you just couldn't wait to grow up, stop being held back because of your youth, and live life on your *own* terms? The strange thing is the older most of us get, the less we actually *live*.

We allow negative thoughts to infiltrate our mind, we start putting other people's opinions and happiness above our own, and day by day, we slowly dim our light down until we're frozen, standing in total darkness, afraid and uncertain of where to go next.

Once upon a time you were a little girl with BIG dreams and a vast vision of the fabulous life your future self would live. Don't disappoint her. It's not too late to turn things around and become the woman you've always wanted to be. The truth is it's never too late. Everything you need to go on this journey of personal transformation already resides within you. You are powerful. You are brilliant. You are worthy. You are *ready*.

You can do this.

It's time to step up, rise above your present self, and do something you've never done before.

If you want it bad enough, it is yours.

Are you ready to go all in?

The hardest part is getting started

When it comes to any task, goal, or challenge, the most difficult part is always overcoming our resistance and getting started. From the outside, it looks tough, overwhelming, and uncertain, so our natural instinct is to avoid it and do something easier instead—something we *know* we can accomplish. We're afraid of the unknown, so we push it to the back of our minds thinking we'll come back to it later when we're feeling smarter, stronger, wealthier, happier, or wiser. The trouble is no matter how much time elapses, we never quite feel ready, so we put it off another day.

I waited a few years too long to begin writing and working on my passion projects. I second-guessed myself and didn't truly believe I was good enough or ready to tell the world my story. But guess what I found out? You'll never feel ready. The only way you become good enough is by consistently showing up and working.

There's always a reason to put something off and not do it today. If you're looking for an excuse or a way out, you'll inevitably find one. The trouble is that someday quickly becomes today which turns into yesterday and then *never*. Life is incredibly short and unpredictable—who knows how many more tomorrows each of us will be lucky enough to wake up to?

There are seven days in the week, and *someday* is definitely not one of them.

There is no better time than *right now* to get started on changing your life.

Let's do this, glow getter!

GLOW

GUIDE

#GLOWGETTERTRIBE

WHY do I want to transform my life?

The power of affirmations

An affirmation is simply an embellished word for a positive thought that you repeat out loud which describes your goal in its already completed state. I like to think of them as a workout for your *mind*. They're central to The Law Of Attraction (the idea that what you think about is what you end up magnetically attracting into your life) and creating the life of your dreams, and can have profound effects in reshaping your inner beliefs and attitudes that may have been holding you back from your goals all this time.

Many people use affirmations as a way to stay focused on their goals and to navigate through any obstacles that arise along the way. What I love most about them is they help to create higher vibrations of happiness, gratitude, joy, bliss, and love, which in turn helps you to attract people, resources, and opportunities into your life that will help you reach your goals and live your dream life.

How to create your own affirmations

1. Choose a negative thought you often find yourself thinking, e.g. *"My life sucks."*

2. Write down that negative thought on a piece of paper, then tear it up and throw it away!

3. Find a more *positive* opposite to that thought. Instead of replacing *"My life sucks,"* with *"My life doesn't suck,"* you will say, *"I am so grateful to be living a beautiful and abundant life."*

4. Repeat that affirmation ten to twenty times in one sitting daily, or throughout your day, so that positive thought becomes embedded in your mind.

A couple of things to remember:

- ♥ Always start with the powerful words *"I am."*
- ♥ Use the present tense.
- ♥ Keep it positive—state what you want, not what you don't want.
- ♥ Keep it brief, but get really specific.
- ♥ Include an action word ending with –ing.
- ♥ Affirmations are personal and only work for you, not others, so allow yourself to be self-indulgent and keep it about you.

Your mission today: Light a candle, find a sacred space of calm, pick out your favourite pen, and create three of your very own affirmations. Make sure these affirm your achievements of your three most important goals or dreams, and then commit to a time each day when you'll practice these.

A sticky note on the fridge or a reminder on your phone will ensure you don't forget, even on days when you're rushed off your feet.

You can also head to **shanijay.com/glowguide** to download your free workbook that includes a worksheet for this chapter's Glow Guide, along with all the others in this book!

BULLSHIT, YOU AREN'T LIVING

"I think too many people lay down in a life they don't love and go, 'Well, I guess I'm here so... fuck it, I'll just stay'... You aren't doing anybody a favor when you stop living, stop trying. When we heal our suffering, we heal this world. When we do what we love, we heal this world."

— Janne Robinson

Everybody always asks what you do for a living, if you've got a house, if you're married, if you have kids—as if life is some kind of a grocery list. But no one ever asks us if we're *happy*.

Most people are settling for ordinary

Why do we often set our sights low? We aim for average. We get okay with mediocre. We stop wanting to win. We happily stand on the sidelines watching other people race towards their finish lines.

It's human nature to avoid change. We crave comfort, the known, and stability. It's in our DNA to shy away from risk and all things unfamiliar. As soon as we begin school, gradually over the years, our creativity, confidence, and self-belief are shaken out of us.

It's the outside world that teaches us how to be human—what's deemed acceptable and what's not. From childhood we are punished or rewarded according to our "good" or "bad" behaviour. That craving for a reward doesn't disappear and we're afraid of being punished, so we pretend to be someone we're not in order to please others—our parents, our school teachers, our friends, and our colleagues. We pretend because we're afraid of being rejected, which in turn snowballs into the fear of not being good enough, and before we know it, we've become a shadow of who we truly are at heart.

And that is exactly how we become stuck. We hate our crappy nine-to-five job, but we like taking home that monthly paycheck, so we suck it up and carry on. We're not happy in our relationship, but we're scared of being on our own because it's been so long we've almost forgotten what that feels like. We desperately want to change our circumstances, but we're so caught up in what others might say that we are afraid of being rejected by those around us. We know we're not living the life we're meant to be living, but we have no idea how to change it and it's easier not to try.

So we stay put.

We don't listen to what our hearts are signalling us. We fail to believe in ourselves, and instead we accept the current hand we've been dealt. We plod on and before we realise it, another year has passed us by. We forget that we only get so many of these years.

Take a look around you. How many people are settling? In a job, a relationship, or in falling short of the person they have the potential to be?

I see it every single day and it makes my heart bleed to see so many people swallowing their truth.

Before I quit my job, I used to be surrounded by a sea of people like this. People who pretended like they'd been dealt a good hand. People who convinced themselves they enjoyed their life. People who needed those fat paychecks every month so they could buy shit they didn't need and get parole every once in a while to go on a sunny holiday for the four weeks a year they're allowed out of their prison. They convince themselves that it's worth it and they're happy. But they're *not*. If I had to sit myself down and draw a picture of someone who's happy, they wouldn't even come close.

Be honest with yourself right now—are *you* settling?

And if you are, why do you think that is?

Maybe deep down, you don't believe you're deserving of better. But trust me when I tell you you're just as deserving as anybody else. You were born to live your truth and do your heart's work.

Perhaps you're stuck in your job right now because it pays the bills and takes care of your family, and hey, we've all gotta put a roof over our heads somehow. I get that, but what about the rest of your time? The hours of 5 a.m. - 8 a.m. before you get there? 7 p.m. - 12 a.m. when you're home? And then there's your weekends of course. What are you doing with the rest of your time to make sure you're living your *best* life?

Forget the bills, your house, your responsibilities, and your relationship status for a second—what are you doing to make *yourself* happy?

Don't waste more than half your life being miserable

Now, I'm definitely not just talking about *work* when I talk about settling, but work is a biggie because it does take up a lot of our time whether we want it to or not—especially in the early days when we're just getting started. What I've noticed from speaking to many women—friends and total strangers—is the biggest complaint on most people's list is their *work*.

Why do we keep doing things we hate?

On average, most people spend around 35-40 hours working each week. That's a lot of time to spend being miserable and hating your existence, right?

You've gotta ask yourself is it *worth* it? Is that paycheck at the end of the month worth you trading in your happiness? Are you satisfied with the work you're doing every day? Is your fancy car, your house, and your wardrobe enough to keep you living this way?

Are you going to get to the end of your life, look back, and think you spent your time wisely?

I was hustling on the side of my day job so that I could eventually make my side hustle my *main* hustle and quit, but you might not want your own business and that's okay—that life isn't for everyone. What I'm saying is don't stick with a job that makes you want to vomit when you wake up Monday morning. If you're not happy with where your life is heading, *do* something about it because nobody else will. The fact that you're even awake should fill you with joy and excitement and make you want to leap out of bed and face the day. So many people weren't lucky enough to wake up yesterday or today and many more won't be tomorrow.

Let that sink in for a moment.

Life is fleeting. It comes and goes in a flash. At the end of your time here, you want to be able to look back on your life and know that every day you spent on this earth was filled with the work of your *heart*. Not the work of somebody else's.

Maybe you *think* you don't know what your true passion is. But that's probably not the case. Deep down, you *know* what lights you up, what you love talking about or doing, the worlds in which you spend a lot of your free time escaping in. I don't mean when you're sprawled out watching crappy TV; I mean the activities you do where you feel at *home*. Maybe it's baking spectacular cakes, writing, or rocking out at music festivals—think about what you spend a lot of your free time on, often unknowingly.

Do you have it?

Good.

Now do more of it. Do it every single day. "Busy" is just an excuse we tell ourselves when we're not prepared to find the time. I know you can carve out at least 10 minutes each day to spend time doing something you truly love. Run with it. Throw your all into it. See what happens and where it takes you.

The heart wants what it wants. You won't ever reach a state of true happiness until you listen to your heart's whispers.

You're allowed to change

At the very young age of 18, the majority of us are forced to make a decision on what career path we want to take. You might not have realised the gravity of it at the time, but you were making a decision on what you wanted to do for the *rest of your life*. That's awfully young to be deciding on your entire future, don't you think?

Yes, you can change your mind, but most people don't, even when they desperately want to because this quickly becomes all we know and what we're most comfortable with. The prospect of changing appears too challenging and messy. So we suck it up and keep going, and all that does is compromise our future happiness.

When you think about who you are now compared to who you were at 16 or 18 or even 21, you've probably changed and grown a lot— more than you might even realise on the surface. Your interests, your priorities, and even your personality. We all change, some of us more so than others.

This is often the case in friendships and romantic relationships too. When we form those initial bonds and partnerships, we might still be teenagers or young adults. Over the years we go through multiple transformations and find ourselves naturally forming new relationships with people who are more aligned with who and where we are *today*.

Even though it's painful and sometimes heartbreaking, we have to let certain people go so that we can fully move forward and continue on the path we're supposed to travel down. Occasionally, we cling on because we can't bear the thought of letting go, but eventually we must find a way to because that relationship is no longer serving and nurturing our soul the way it used to.

Remember—you're allowed to change. In fact, it's imperative that you do.

At 17, I decided I wanted to be a fashion designer. So I stopped putting effort into my other subjects at school and affirmed to myself that fashion was all that mattered. I went on to study fashion design at university for the next three years, and to begin with I *loved* it. It was exciting, it was stimulating, and it allowed me to constantly be creative. However, there was a part of me that began to question what good I was doing by choosing this career. Who was I helping? Was I making a positive impact in my world?

At the end of my second year, I had to begin researching for my dissertation which meant regular trips to the library and lots of reading, which I've enjoyed doing my entire life. During this time, I unknowingly began to fall in love with writing, and it ended up being an escape for me from the crazy fashion world which I spent the rest of my time immersed in. After writing the dissertation, I knew that something wasn't right. I shouldn't have enjoyed it that much in comparison to what I was doing for the other 70% of my time while at uni—but I did.

Like most people do, I buried my head in the sand and ignored what my heart was signalling to me because how on earth was I going to forge a career in writing now as I'd just spent the past three years learning how to design and make *clothes*? So I carried on down the rabbit hole and got my first job as a designer abroad in Sri Lanka. At first, I loved it (mostly because I was getting to explore an exotic country where my roots are—I'm half Sri-Lankan—and it felt like I was on holiday most of the time!), but six months later I made the decision to move back home because, in my heart of hearts, I knew this just wasn't where I was supposed to be.

I then fell into a job as a trainee fashion buyer and almost immediately began to hate everything about my job and therefore hate my life. *Urgh.* It might sound all kinds of glamorous to you, and while it certainly wasn't the worst job in the world, it crippled me from the inside out. I'm sure you can resonate with that feeling. There was so much admin, spreadsheets, doing math (I *didn't* sign up for that), and a tonne of bitchy women. I felt trapped, and I couldn't see a way out.

So I carried on for the next three years trying to convince myself that this was a good career with progression and that in the grand scheme of things it was a pretty exciting job to have—a job I know so many girls only dream of having. But I was lying to myself, and deep down I knew that I was miserable and something had to change and *fast*.

As you already know, I then re-discovered my passion for writing and decided to pursue it in my spare time, all the while trying to figure out how I could turn it into a career. I didn't give up even when I wasn't getting the yes's I wanted and I was only earning pennies. I didn't for a moment allow myself to be held back by internal fears, worries, or the fact that I had spent the past *10 years* building a career in the fashion industry. If I had, you wouldn't be reading this book right now!

As bestselling author Danielle Steel says:

> *"Never settle for less than your dreams, somewhere, sometime, someday, somehow, you'll find them."*

My message to you is this: it's more than okay to wake up one day and decide you want to live a different life because the one you've woken up to isn't making you truly happy. It's okay to switch careers, to end a ten-year relationship, and to decide you're going to take off the label that you've worn for so long.

You must quit the life you hate in order to start *living*.

Never allow fear of the unknown or fear of judgement to keep you from living your truth. For that is all you came here to do.

We are living in an incredible time—don't waste it

Thanks to the internet and the invention of social media, we are presented with a world of open doors and opportunities our parents and grandparents could only *dream* of.

Back in their day, every industry was ruled by its own gatekeepers, and in order to push your way in, you had to go through them. Social media was nonexistent, so the numbers of people you could connect with were restricted, and you had to go through traditional costly forms of advertising (radio, newspapers, TV) in order to reach the masses.

What took weeks or even months to achieve back then can be completed in seconds or minutes today thanks to significant advances in technology. If you want to become a scuba diver on the other side of the world, you can find a training course today and book your plane ticket. If you want to make music, you can record yourself singing and instantly upload it where it can then potentially be watched and shared by millions of people online. If you want to start a handmade jewellery business from your bedroom, there is absolutely *nothing* standing in your way.

There is no way I would've been able to reach the same amount of people back then as I have with my writing, my books, and my message today. Websites didn't exist and it took a long time before they became user-friendly and easy to design and create yourself. Self-publishing didn't exist either, and your only hope of writing and publishing a book was to be picked up by one of the select publishing houses—and the chances of that happening were slim.

We are incredibly fortunate to be living in a time where we can turn what we love and what we're most passionate about into a career. You no longer have to wait around—which you might've done in gym class like I did!—for someone to pick you. You can pick yourself. You can be and do *anything* you want. Everything is yours for the taking.

Please, don't waste this gift.

And remember, this life-changing journey can be everything you want it to be—it all comes down to how you choose to see it.

When you think of turning your dreams into reality, what do you imagine? Hard work, sacrifice, obstacles, discipline, and courage? Or do you instead choose to picture great adventures, magic in the most unexpected places, side-splitting laughter, beautiful surprises, fulfilling relationships, and experiencing a whole new world? Your chosen perspective has the power to change *everything* about your onward journey and where you decide to go from here.

If you're not happy with where you're currently headed, be brave enough to change directions. Do not be afraid to step off the path that everyone else is walking blindly on.

You were not born to live the life of somebody else or to follow in the footsteps of others. You are here to go your own way. Your wildest dreams are one of a kind, just like you are.

If you find yourself without a deep desire to wake up each morning and begin your day, refuse to accept that as the norm. Don't deal in mediocre when I know you were born to live a passionate life filled with adventure, magic, and the unexpected.

The only person who knows what's truly best for you is *you*. Have the courage to honour what your heart is whispering to you.

GLOW

GUIDE

In what parts of your life do you think you're settling today?

Find your passion

Write a list of all the things you love doing—y'know, the things that make time go by super fast and fuel you with energy and passion.

I love...

Your dream life in pictures

In January 2016, I decided to make the very first vision board for myself for the year ahead. If you haven't heard of it, a vision board is simply a beautiful collection of images, words, and maybe even objects that are meaningful to you, and what you hope to accomplish in your year ahead.

Regardless what time of year it is, it's always the perfect time to start a new vision! It's super fun too—you get to rifle through gorgeous magazines and tear out images and quotes that inspire you, and have a good old Pinterest scroll too. You could even do your own doodles and drawings, and make sure to include your affirmations.

Your mission today: Create your own vision board that fills you with love the moment you set eyes upon it. I like to put a happy playlist on and set a whole evening aside to do this because it's so enjoyable! Get yourself a large pinboard or piece of cardboard, and go to town on it! Fill it with images and words that light you up, what you're dreaming of manifesting in your life, and anything that your heart is magnetically drawn to.

Be sure to place it somewhere you know you'll see it every single day so you can be inspired by the life you're in the midst of creating for yourself. Surrounding yourself with your dreams and goals serves as a wonderful reminder of what you're trying to accomplish; it helps to keep you motivated and pushes you closer towards a happier and healthier you.

Head to **shanijay.com/glowguide** to download your master Glow Guide for free, which contains all the other guides in this book, plus lots of extra surprises!

MINDSET IS EVERYTHING

"You carry both lightning and thunder in that space between your bones and soul. Become the storm you are hiding from, a hurricane does not run from the rain."

— Nikita Gill

You've probably come across the saying, *"What we think, we become,"* and this entire chapter can be summarised by those five powerful words. If you take away just one thing from this section, let it be this! Before you can transform your life, you have to get yourself into the right mindset that will aid your transformation and become a powerful tool you can call upon when life gets a little rocky.

Maybe you should go and love yourself...

The term "self-love" can seem all kinds of fluffy, especially because it's thrown around so much these days. To love yourself essentially means having a strong regard for your own well-being and happiness. If you're familiar with my writing and previous books, you'll know just how strongly I feel about self-love. It's so important that I felt compelled to write a whole book on it!

As women, we often struggle balancing the time we spend caring for others, alongside the time we spend caring for ourselves. We have this bad habit of putting everyone else first, and before we know it, the clock reads midnight and what *we* wanted to do (take a bubble bath, go to that spin class, spend 30 minutes journaling) gets pushed back to tomorrow because we failed to prioritise our *own* needs.

Your wants and needs matter, and they definitely shouldn't wind up at the bottom of the list. Of course, life happens and you have certain commitments and responsibilities to stick to. Perhaps you're a stay-at-home mum raising a young family, or you're in the early years of running your own business and are spinning ten plates at once. But in order to become your best self, regardless of what little time you have each day, it's important to make *your* happiness a priority and understand what that truly means. You might think that means being selfish and blindly ignoring your other duties, but that's simply not the case. It's all about finding a healthy balance.

Learning to love who you are and making time for self-care is the rock-solid foundation for your dream life and all that you've been craving. If you don't work on loving yourself first, you won't be able to make the right choices that align with the woman you aspire to *be*. The truth is that every aspect of your life affects every other aspect of your life. You can't separate your job, your relationships, or your personal life because they all have a significant impact on each other.

Ever since I was a teenager, self-love and confidence were two of the biggest things I struggled with. Luckily, my weight has never been an issue for me, but I did have a hard time becoming comfortable in my own skin and feeling good about myself. Being a shy Asian girl attending a predominantly white school immediately made me stand out without me having to say a word, since as you know, kids will find any kind of weakness or difference to single you out.

I didn't realise it at the time, but this had a knock-on effect on *everything*—my self-esteem, being able to stand up and speak up for myself, my self-respect, my self-worth, going after what I wanted, and my general day-to-day mood. I constantly felt like I somehow wasn't measuring up to all of the other girls around me which in turn made me feel unworthy of anything *good*. I was incredibly unhappy, and after leaving school, those negative feelings stayed with me for years after because I had no idea how to change them, and it saddens me to know that there are so many young girls and women who feel exactly the same way.

You might not know it, but the limit to your self-abuse is equivalent to the limit you're willing to tolerate from others. So if someone abuses you *more* than you abuse yourself, you'll walk away from them, but if they abuse you a little *less* than you do, you're likely to continue that relationship because deep down you believe you deserve it—but you don't.

Here lies the reason why some of us continue to attract and date assholes. As soon as I learned to love and value myself and my own opinion over the opinion of men, I stopped dating losers who weren't treating me with the respect and love I knew I deserved. And you deserve that too, beautiful. As soon as I had that epiphany and shift in my heart, it made room for an amazing man to walk into my life—and he did.

The more love you nurture within your heart and show yourself, the less you'll abuse yourself and finally begin to feel at peace. It took me the best part of 10 years to transform my mindset and learn to love and *celebrate* who I am, inside and out. There's no overnight fix and I still have the occasional moment where I get stuck playing the comparison game and fail to recognise everything that's beautiful about me and my life, but now I make a conscious effort to stop and see the sparkle within my soul and notice the glitter running through my veins. Don't wait for someone else to discover your true magic before you begin to embrace it.

I *finally* realised that I'm a fabulous cosmic miracle—and so are you!

So start living like it, okay?

There's an endless number of ways you can start to infuse your life with more love and nurture your mind, body, and soul, starting today:

- ♥ Look in the mirror each day and give yourself a compliment.
- ♥ Write yourself a love letter, and re-read it anytime you need a little boost.
- ♥ Dress in outfits that make you feel like a Goddess (matching lingerie helps a tonne and it's just so pretty!).
- ♥ Treat yourself to fresh flowers every now and then just 'cos.
- ♥ Pour yourself a luxurious bubble bath with relaxing salts, candles, and a glass of wine.
- ♥ Surround yourself with people who make you feel *good* and lift your spirits.
- ♥ Do something nice for someone you love.
- ♥ Cook yourself a delicious, healthy meal from scratch.

- Make a list of all the things that make you AWESOME (you can't stop until you've got at least 20!!).
- Spend some time reading books on self-love and soaking up expert knowledge and tips.
- Stand up for yourself and what you believe in.
- Turn your favourite song up, and just DANCE!
- Set aside at least 30 minutes each day to do something just for *you*.
- Get rid of all the clutter in your home and make it your very own serene sanctuary.
- Spend some time journaling all your thoughts, feelings, and ideas.

I wish I could tell you there's a magic potion or overnight fix, but there's *not*. Learning to love yourself takes time. It's about waking up each day and showing yourself the love and care you deserve—especially on days when you're struggling to feel worthy of it. In time, that love will begin to bloom.

Try and do at least one of these every day, and it won't be long before you begin to notice the difference in how lifted, positive, and happy you feel within your heart.

Believe in yourself

You are no longer a child; no one can tell you what to do or who to be. It's up to you to decide what to believe in—start with believing in *yourself*.

In order to make real, transformational changes in your life, you have to first *believe* that you're capable of making those changes and sticking to your new and improved daily habits, especially when the universe decides (and you *know* it will) to throw a gigantic asteroid your way and flip your world upside down.

What I know for certain is you will encounter challenges—in the shape of events as well as people—along your journey to your best self that will make you question who you are and what you're doing. You might find yourself thinking along the lines of:

Everyone thinks I'm going to fail, and I probably will.
I've never succeeded before, so why will this be different?
This is going to be really tough, and I might not be able to do it...
Who am I to think I can change my life?

This is how most people think, and it's also the reason why most people fail. They don't believe in themselves. They allow negative voices to take over their minds. Listen up, sister—if *you* don't believe in yourself, who the hell else will? No one is on their way to save you—everything is now up to you.

Who are you to think you *can't* change your life?

Why can't you? Take a look around you. Plenty of women have already stood up and taken responsibility for their own happiness and future and have totally transformed their lives. There is nothing stopping you from being one of those glow getters too. You simply have to believe that it's possible. Believing is half of the battle you're fighting.

Your life will be full of people trying to convince you that you can't do something. Pay them no attention. They are simply trying to inflict their own lack of self-belief onto you. Learn to be your own cheerleader, even when everyone else walks away.

I believe in you, beautiful. It's about time you started believing too.

Think positive

There was a time in my life when I was awfully negative about myself and life in its entirety too. I'd always think the worst was going to happen in any situation I found myself in, and I convinced myself that I must've simply been born with a case of bad luck. When anything unfortunate did happen, I'd allow myself to get carried away down a negative spiral and tell myself things were far worse than in reality.

I'd watch other people around me finding their way to great things, achieving plenty of success, and living what appeared to be a much happier existence than the one I was living. Why did life never go my way? Why couldn't I find great friends, a fulfilling job, or an awesome boyfriend? Woe was definitely me—I can *almost* hear the violins playing in the background as I write this!

But this was all simply an illusion that I created in my mind. I didn't have bad luck. In fact, when I think about it now, I was extremely blessed with the life I lived. I had my health, I never had to go through the pain of losing somebody close to me, I had a great education, I was born in a country that meant I had equal rights as a woman—rights that other women can only dream of— and I was born to parents who loved and cared for me deeply. I was living the kind of life that some people merely *dream* of and I still managed to convince myself I'd been dealt a poor hand.

Chances are you wouldn't believe any of that if you met me today because now I'm usually the one that helps other people find the silver lining in their rain clouds. I'm the bright and cheery optimist who tells people everything's going to be okay.

Isn't it strange how much we have the capacity to evolve as people?

You might believe that each of us are born optimists or pessimists and that we have to then live the rest of our lives thinking that way, but that's far from the truth. We have the power to change what and how we think. We possess the power to transform our mindset and imagine *better*.

Thoughts become your reality so you must think amazing ones! How many times a day do you think you whisper something negative to yourself? Pay attention to your thought process today and keep count—you might find those negative thoughts automatically popping into your head more often than you think they do. When you think negatively, you're unknowingly attracting negative energy into your life, and you're using up your precious mind space on bad vibes—space which you could be filling with good vibrations that would help you feel lighter, happier, and ready to take on anything.

Most people believe they need to have more money or time before they can begin living their dream life and finally be happy and at peace. But we've got this backwards! First and foremost, you've gotta learn to be happy and grateful with what you've got right now, begin working on those dreams from your happy place, and you'll naturally attract more of those things you wanted in the first place.

Negative thinking is a bad habit that's incredibly easy to fall into and much harder to climb back out of, but it's totally possible. First of all, you need to make yourself *aware* of those negative thoughts and notice when they creep into your mind. When they do, don't give them the time of day. I find it sometimes helps to picture yourself grabbing that thought out of your mind and throwing it in the garbage! Next, you need to replace that negative thought with a fabulous one. It helps to make it the opposite of the negative thought you just had.

For example, you might find yourself thinking, *"I'm not going to be able to do this,"* and a great replacement would be along the lines of, **"I am a strong and confident woman who can accomplish anything I set my mind to."** Another common thought might be based on your physical appearance such as, *"Why would anyone find me attractive?"* which would become, **"I am beautiful inside and out."**

It might feel alien at first and difficult to find a positive replacement thought because you're so used to living inside that toxic cage of negativity we're breaking you out of, but stick with this practice and pay attention to how your thoughts begin to transform.

Thinking positive in your mind is one thing, but it's also imperative that you surround yourself with other positive people who are aligned with your way of thinking. Have you ever heard of the saying, you are the product of the five people you spend the most time with? Well, that saying is gospel. If you surround yourself with people who think and behave in a negative fashion, constantly criticise other people, and bitch and moan about their life but don't do a damn thing to change it, that negative energy is going to rub off on you, no matter how hard you try and ignore it.

We're going to discuss this in more detail in a later chapter, but for now, take a long hard look around you and the people you've invited into your world. Are they helping you to grow and become your best self or are they only holding you back?

Quit comparing yourself to others

Your journey is one of a kind, just like you are. Everything in your past has been leading up to where you find yourself standing right at this very moment. Everything that has happened to you happened for good reason.

You might find your eyes and mind wandering and see people who are much further ahead in their journey than you are.

Sound familiar? Yeah, I've been there too, and I want you to know that's okay. Feeling jealous is something we all experience in our lives. We see someone living a beautiful life, one that we merely dream of, and we can't help but feel a pang inside ourselves that wonders, *"Why can't I have that? Why is she successful? Why is she able to live out her dreams and I'm stuck here?"*

All you must remember is her journey is not *yours*, and you are exactly where you need to be right now. Never compare yourself to other people because we are all so very different, and we are all here to accomplish and triumph at different things.

Don't get me wrong—pushing yourself and striving for more is great. Being ambitious and motivated is the only way to find success—but don't involve other women. There's no need, and there's plenty of success to go around.

The invention and explosion of social media has meant that each day we're bombarded with beautiful, "flawless" images of women travelling the world, getting paid to take pretty photos of themselves dolled up in buckets of makeup and designer clothes (or not many clothes at all)—essentially living what we believe to be an easy and awesome existence. Everything appears to be so much easier for *them* and a painful struggle for *us*, but we forget we can't see behind closed doors. Nobody has everything.

Aside from the celebs and insta-famous women, we might find ourselves looking at people we know or used to know doing fabulous things while we feel stuck in exactly the same place we were a few years ago. Marissa lost ten stone and looks insanely good; Yasmine married a gorgeous millionaire, moved to sunny Australia, and just had a baby; and Lauren quit her job to start her own online business which is thriving, and she now posts photos of herself working from the beach in Costa Rica, sipping on jaguar coladas.

If scrolling through Facebook or Instagram is doing nothing but make you feel un-pretty, un-worthy, or jealous, then why do you continue to allow it into your life? If a *man* was making you feel that way, I'm sure you'd tell him where the hell to go, and this is no different. If you know deep down something isn't good for you, be brave enough to remove it from your life. What do we really gain from social media anyway? All it does is take away at least 30 minutes each day we could be spending doing something we truly love.

Don't look at what other women have and where they are and wish you could swap places. Don't put yourself in competition with a woman who has something you're dreaming of because *your* path is not hers. Encourage yourself to be better each day, better than you were yesterday, but take no notice of those around you. Be inspired by other women and what they have accomplished, and be happy for them and their success. Be mindful that your life won't change overnight. Learn to be patient with yourself and remember you are playing the long game.

This transformational journey that you're on is about YOU and bettering *yourself*. Don't involve anyone else. Never compare yourself to anyone but you because at the end of the day, you are the only person you need to make proud.

GLOW

GUIDE

Inhale sunshine and rainbows, exhale the bullshit

The moment I found meditation, I fell head over heels for it. Don't be afraid of it if you've never tried it before; it's not the weird, hippy dippy, religious chanting ritual you might think it is! Meditating is simply the art of sitting peacefully in a chair, or cross-legged on the floor, and doing nothing but breathing deeply. Even if you only dedicate five minutes a day to it, it can work wonders for your mind, body, and soul. I find I'm always instantly calmed, energised, and more positive after meditating. There are some great apps like Calm and Headspace to help you if you're a total beginner.

When you breathe in, imagine yourself inhaling positive energy, good thoughts, and loving kindness. And when you breathe out, release all of the pain, anger, resentment, jealousy, and feelings of unworthiness that plague your mind and body.

Journal your thoughts on how you feel after doing this exercise.

Make a list of all the things you love about yourself

(Don't stop until you've got at least 10!)

♥

♥

♥

♥

♥

♥

♥

♥

♥

♥

♥

♥

♥

♥

If you want more love in your life...

Head on over to **shanijay.com/glowgetter** and take part in the self-love sanctuary—a fun 7-day challenge—for free today!

YOUR BIGGEST ADVENTURE YET

"Anytime I feel lost, I pull out a map and stare. I stare until I have reminded myself that life is a giant adventure, so much to do, to see."

— Angelina Jolie

I distinctly remember being on a solo holiday in Sri Lanka in November 2015 for my friend's wedding and realising that I needed to do something drastic to change my life because I couldn't continue on blindly through the hazy fog I found myself trapped in. I knew I wasn't doing what I was put on this earth to do, but I had no idea what that was, or perhaps deep down I *did* know, but I wasn't ready to admit it to myself because that would be terrifying and I'd have to finally jump off the conveyor belt I was on and actually start doing something about it!

While on a short Christmas break that same year, I decided to write something for fun and submit it to a site called *Thought Catalog*, which I'd been reading for almost three years at that point but never thought I was a good enough writer to even be considered. But something within me thought, you know what, *fuck it*, I'm gonna try and see what happens because a girl's gotta start somewhere. About two weeks later, I found an email in my inbox saying, "*Your submission has been accepted.*" And as minor as it seems, it was in that moment that everything changed.

Not all those who wander are *lost*

Something strange happens when you remove yourself from your everyday life and give your mind time and space to wander freely. Suddenly, as if by magic, you'll be able to see clearly with a newfound sense of clarity. Inspiration and epiphanies will flow to you with ease, and everything that seemed so damn complicated before will appear plain and simple.

I find I *always* do my best thinking while on holiday—despite never intentionally planning it that way. Something about the air encourages me to breathe deeper, my senses are stirred, my mind is both at peace yet more *awake* than it ever has been. My soul comes *alive*, and I feel deeply connected to my heartsong and my purpose here on earth.

Our everyday lives are nothing but go, go, go—often we don't even stop to take a breath and notice where we are or what we're doing. Escaping for a few days, a few weeks, or even a few months (if your circumstances allow it!) and dedicating that time solely to *yourself* can truly help you to regain perspective on your current life and make perfect sense of the senseless stuff!

If you find yourself stuck inside your head feeling confused, lost, and unsure of where to go next, I highly recommend you plan a solo getaway for *one*. It doesn't matter if you head to the local countryside or if you travel to an exotic island on a different continent. It doesn't matter how long you go for or whether you end up going in coach or first class. What matters is that you go alone, and you go somewhere you've always dreamed of going. Maybe to you that's a long spa weekend in Iceland, a few weeks on a secluded tropical beach doing yoga and detoxing, or a week sailing and sunning in the Mediterranean. If it's something you can't afford right now, start putting away a little each week towards it and plan when you'll be able to go.

This is your time to explore, wander, and allow yourself to revel in the feeling of being lost in an unknown town, city, or country.

Don't look at this as a frivolous holiday because it's *not*—this is a journey for your heart, a journey for your soul. This is you giving yourself permission to follow your dreams. This is you finding what lights you up. This is you reaffirming to yourself that you *matter*, and you are here for a reason. There's no time like the present to figure out what that reason is.

Begin quietly, but with intention

It can be overwhelming going through extreme life changes and starting a new journey. The two biggest things that most of us fear are fear of failure and fear of the unknown. So ask yourself, what is it that you're most afraid of? Then ask yourself, is the mere *possibility* of living your best life worth the temporary discomfort of facing those fears?

If your answer is yes, then it's time to slip on your most fabulous pair of stilettos and get started. It doesn't matter if you have no idea where to begin, just do *something*. Start writing, painting, cooking, dating, doing yoga, taking photos, meditating, volunteering, running, belly dancing, making clothes—whatever helps to add joy and light to your life. The hardest part is getting started—trust me.

Whether you know exactly what it is you want or not, it doesn't matter. What matters is you begin exploring what you might want to do more of, what brings you the most joy, and the most fulfillment. In time, you will find your way to your calling, and once you do you must do all that you can to move closer each day towards it.

Amelia Earhart faced a wealth of adversity and rejection simply for being a woman who wanted to work in aviation back in the 1920s, when people still labelled women as weak and inferior to men. Several years after deciding she couldn't make a living as a pilot and taking a job as a social worker in order to earn her way, she received an unexpected call. It was an offer to go on the first female-funded transatlantic flight, but she would be chaperoned by two men who would be paid well while she would receive *nothing*. Oh, and they also kindly let her know she wasn't their first choice either.

But you know what? She said *yes*. Because that was an opportunity for her to pursue what she loved. She took the opening she was given, and although it wasn't favourable, she never gave up and kept moving forward.

Less than five years later, she became the first female pilot to fly solo nonstop across the Atlantic Ocean.

The lesson is we've all gotta start somewhere; what's important is that we *do* start. Even if that means starting small. That might mean writing for just 10 minutes each day, ensuring you eat one healthy meal a day, or giving yourself one genuine compliment each morning before you head to work. Who knows where you'll be in a month, a year, or 10 years?

There's an old Chinese proverb I love that says, "*The best time to plant a tree was 20 years ago. The second best time is now.*"

Don't worry about being too old or too young or wishing you'd started transforming your life five or ten years ago. That time is now in the past—let it go and concentrate on your present. Don't waste all of the precious time you have left.

Start today, and don't be afraid to start small.

There is no road map for where you are headed

Your journey of self-transformation promises to be bumpy and at times uncomfortable along the way, so take some time to mentally prepare yourself for what lies ahead. Like all adventures, there will be excitement and awe awaiting you, but also the unknown to contend with. You knew this wasn't going to be easy, but I promise you it will be worth it.

Much of the time, people think they need to have their entire lives mapped out for the next 10 years with super specific goals they need to tick off along the way. What they don't realise is life doesn't work that way. It's messy, unpredictable, and constantly surprising us. You don't have to have your entire journey figured out or know exactly where you're going to go. If you do, *great*, but most of us don't and that's okay too. We are ever-evolving, and our desires and dreams can change drastically over time. That's one of the big reasons why so many couples fall in and then back out of love.

Often they grow into two very different people than the ones who initially fell in love.

Don't worry about having your whole journey planned out. Follow what lights you up, what makes you excited to race out of bed each morning, and it won't be long before your heart begins to speak to you.

Remember, whatever it is that you want in the end—more laughter, more dancing, more beautiful sunrises—is what you need to focus on bringing into your life along the journey. That's the only way they'll be there in the end because the process *is* the end—what you do along the way ultimately becomes where you go. So be sure to infuse your whole journey with all of the goodness, the feelings, and the experiences you crave most—at no point will they magically manifest their way into your life without you actively attracting them in.

When I first began writing, I had no idea where it would take me or where I was ultimately hoping to go. I'd always had a lofty dream of writing and publishing a book since I was a little girl, but that wasn't even on my radar when I started writing. I did it because without fail it would always put me on a happy high, and I'd be buzzing for the rest of the day.

The more I did it, the more I loved it, so the more I did it, and everything slowly spiralled from there. Even today, I don't have a clear plan for the next five years of my life, and I think when you do it can often stop you from paying attention to all of the unexpected wonders life gifts you along the way. It can mean you become so focused on an end goal that you forget to enjoy the journey and go with what your gut is telling you.

There will be a tonne of trial and error along the way. What starts out being incredibly important to you might lose its appeal after a few months. So don't be afraid to try many things along the way and just be open to seeing what happens. Life will probably end up surprising you.

Chances are you will find yourself travelling a certain way on your own path and eventually meeting with what *appears* to be a dead end. You won't know which way to go or how you're going to continue moving forwards. When you're on a spiritual journey like this, there are likely to be challenges and obstacles in your way, each one teaching you a valuable lesson or imparting wisdom that you need in order to progress forward. Don't give up. If you can't see a clear path ahead, be confident enough in yourself to know that you can pave your own.

I hope you're excited, glow getter, because this journey promises to be your grandest adventure yet.

GLOW

GUIDE

Retreat yo'self!

Like I mentioned in this chapter, I think we do our very best thinking when we give ourselves time and space away from our everyday lives.

What better way is there to do that than taking yourself on a mini-retreat?!

Depending on the time you have and what you can afford, I want you to plan some solo time away for yourself. You could stay in your home country or travel 5,000 miles across the world; take a few days or take a few weeks—it's completely up to you!

You could book into a yoga or meditation retreat, take a spa weekend, a short city break, or spend the entire time chilling and surfing on the beach—whatever will bring you the most joy.

Be sure to take a journal with you and make time (an hour or so each morning and evening) to sit and think alone and write all your thoughts, ideas, challenges, struggles, fears, and dreams down in it every day.

I think you'll surprise yourself with the breakthroughs you end up having!

Start a dream jar

A dream jar is a small-ish sized jar that you fill with all of your BIGGEST dreams—everything you want to see happen in your life and everything you're prepared to work for until you finally achieve it.

Your mission: Get a stack of scrap pieces of colourful paper, sticky notes, or whatever you like. Write down all of your biggest and boldest dreams separately, fold each one up, and pop it in your dream jar. Make a point of picking them out randomly now and then and read them to yourself as a reminder of what you're working towards. And once you make a dream come true, take it out of the jar and pin it up somewhere as a reminder of what you've achieved.

FYI, it doesn't have to be a *jar*—it can be any kind of pot, mug, or holder as long as it holds your dreams and is pretty to look at (you don't wanna clutter your space with anything that doesn't make you feel good when you look at it).

As always, you can head to **shanijay.com/glowguide** to download a free workbook with all of the Glow Guides from the book, plus a whole lot more!

STEP INTO YOUR NEW STORY

"Step out of the story that is holding you back. Step into the new story you are willing to create."

— Oprah Winfrey

You know what the biggest excuse is for most people not transforming their lives?

Time.

We consistently complain about how there's not enough hours in the day to accomplish what we desire, but do we truly believe that? After all, we're blessed with the very same 24 hours a day that Oprah, Malala, and Beyoncé all have. The only difference between you and them is they decided what was most important to them and devoted their entire lives to following that through to the end. They were laser-focused in their thinking and didn't allow themselves to be swerved off course by *anything*.

Learning to say no to short-term pleasure

Think about how you spend your time in an average week, aside from the necessities like going to work, spending time with your family, household chores, etc. Maybe you sink a few happy hour cocktails with colleagues after work, sleep in on the weekend, or scroll through your Facebook feed to see what's happening, and before you know it, you've spent 45 minutes watching cute panda baby videos on YouTube.

All of these activities are a lot of fun in the moment, there's no denying that, but think about how much time all of those separate things total up to each week. Think about what you *could* be doing with that precious time instead. Before you engage in anything, it helps to ask yourself, is what I'm about to do helping me to transform my life and reach my higher self?

Once I made the decision to pursue a writing career, I knew I had to start making choices that were going to propel me forward on my mission rather than hold me back. I also knew that most people I was surrounded with at work lacked that higher thinking, so I couldn't allow myself to be distracted by their opinions or actions.

I found myself turning down invites to after-work drinks and parties, despite people getting on my case for doing so. I'd get home, and after being up already for more than 13 hours, I would have loved nothing more than to relax in front of the TV, but instead I'd open up my laptop and carry on writing.

I also—like a *lot* of women—used to have such an unhealthy addiction to shopping. Anytime I was happy, sad, angry, or lonely, I'd look to new clothes and shoes to make me feel better—similarly, some people use food as their source of comfort. But I finally had the realisation that this wasn't helping to fix any of my problems, and all my hard-earned money was simply going down the drain— money which could be spent on bettering myself through online courses, books, mentorship, or investing in my business. So over a period of 12 months, I completely stopped shopping. I can't explain what a battle it has been, but it's a battle I'm proud to say I'm currently winning, and that feels awesome!

There was also a time in my life, from about the age of 18 to 25, where I used to love going out and partying. I've always been a bit of a lightweight, so it wouldn't take much before I'd reach that state of drunken euphoria. The next day, I'd be like a zombie of my usual bubbly self, sluggishly going about my day and pretty much wasting the entirety of it due to my careless actions the night before. I'd regret drinking so much, promise myself I'd do better next time, but naturally found myself back in the same old place the following week.

The harsh reality is the majority of us get drunk (or smoke, eat excessively, or stay in toxic relationships) because deep down we don't *like* ourselves and we don't like the lives we have created, so we drink to numb our pain and temporarily forget. We continue to find ways to bruise ourselves when we don't like the reflection staring back at us in the mirror.

In the moment, drinking away all of life's problems was making me feel good, but outside of those couple of hours, drinking excessively like that was only making me feel worse about my life, creating *more* problems, and was stealing precious time away from me. Fortunately, I was never close to being an alcoholic, but like many people, I used to struggle to have just *one* drink, so I finally made the decision to stop saying yes to socialising after work because I could clearly visualise how the evening was likely to pan out. The more I said no, the easier it became each time to say no again.

Today, I love enjoying a large glass of rosé with dinner on a Friday or Saturday evening as an end of the week treat, but I rarely have any more than that because I know it will sap my energy and productivity the following day. My time has now become far more precious to me than anything else. You can always make more money, but you can never buy back *time*.

Naturally, we all need downtime to recharge our batteries, refresh and stimulate our creativity and inspiration, and to reflect and check in with ourselves. Finding the right balance of work and play will keep your motivation from drying up, keep your energy levels high, and stop you from burning out.

No matter how busy I am each day, I still make time to meditate for 10 minutes, to go for a brisk walk and check in with nature or go for a relaxing swim, prepare myself a healthy lunch, and read a book for half an hour before I go to sleep. Occasionally I'll catch up with a girlfriend over dinner, take the evening off and watch a movie, or spend a whole day having quality time with my partner. The difference with all of these activities (compared to getting wasted at the bar) is that they are all serving me in the long run. They aren't centred on short-term joy—they all help me to be a happier and healthier person, inside and out.

In order to grow and become a better person, aligned with what your heart truly wants, it's vital to make short-term sacrifices along the way. It's about looking past the "in the moment" happiness and thinking about the woman you're striving to be in the long run. Before you say *yes* to anything, ask yourself how this will serve you and the future you're trying to create for yourself. If it doesn't align with the woman you desire to be, I want you to remember it's okay to pass on it. It's okay to say no to things and to do what's best for *you* instead of what's best for those around you.

Always look at the bigger picture you're painting.

Insta-fun vs. glow getter fun

Before we delve into this, I want you to know these aren't *official* types of fun—I don't think "types" of fun exist—but this is how I choose to look at it and keep myself focused and motivated on what I *know* is good for me and my future versus what might temporarily feel good in the moment.

Insta-fun refers to any activity that is usually highly enjoyable in the moment and provides instant gratification. This includes relaxing with friends, sunbathing, clubbing, enjoying a few glasses of wine, shopping for new clothes, eating ice cream, having sex, watching a movie, going on vacation, etc. All the things we love to indulge in and often spend much of our free time doing.

Then there's **glow getter fun** which refers to something that can be quite painful and difficult in the moment, but when you look back on it in a few weeks or months, you realise it *was* fun and also extremely rewarding. This could apply to writing a book (there are always a lot of tears, tantrums, and freak-outs in my experience with this one), losing a lot of weight, starting a business, running a marathon, or even learning a new language. By no means are any of these things easy—which is why most people prefer to head straight for insta-fun when they're looking for a pick-me-up or a quick boost of pleasure.

Let's face it—it's far easier to make a groove in the sofa and escape reality for a few hours while you get lost in the fictional lives of the characters you see on TV, but all you're really doing is helping other people become successful while not working on things that are gonna help you reach your *own* dreams.

It's easier to stay in a toxic relationship because it's comfortable and less painful than learning to be on your own and start again from scratch, but it's not good for your heart or your soul or your sanity.

It's easier to stick around in that job from hell because you get a nice paycheck each month which pays for all those fancy dinners and cocktails, new shoes, and vacations in the sun, but you're not being honest with yourself or committing to living a full and beautiful life that you will look back on and be *proud* of.

Now that you know and understand the difference between the two types of fun, you'll be able to recognise those choices you're faced with on a daily basis and commit to making decisions that focus more on your long-term goals instead of only indulging in your short-term desires.

Give a little and you'll gain a *lot*.

You need a routine

What do all of the world's most successful people have in common? They have a routine—a sequence of actions they follow every day which keeps them on track and focused on what they're trying to achieve (both from a personal and business point of view). Once they form their initial routine and begin to put it into practice, it becomes easier each day to stick to it and pretty soon it's on autopilot. What's even more common amongst high achievers is their routine begins in the morning, sometimes as early as 4.30 a.m.

You might be laughing to yourself right now, thinking *"Shani's crazy, how on earth am I going to wake up that early*?!" But if you plan your day right, it's not too difficult. Like all things in this life, it simply depends on how much motivation you have to make bold changes that most people aren't prepared to make. It doesn't matter if you're not usually an early bird—you can train yourself to be one. Persistence and determination will help you to build an early start into your wonderfully new and improved morning routine.

A routine will provide you with the structure and extra time you've probably been struggling to carve out in your day. You'll be able to fill your days with more of what brings you joy, and you won't feel stuck in the rut of waking up, going to work, coming home knackered, sleeping, and then repeating it all over again the next day.

I regularly wake up between 5 and 6 a.m. each morning (apart from one day on the weekend when I have a few extra hours in bed), and I don't feel exhausted. You know why? Because I do my very best to make sure I'm tucked up in my bed by 10 p.m. at the very latest. That's at least 7 hours of sleep each night, and if your body needs more, then get to bed earlier—it's that simple. In fact, I've found that when I sleep in or snooze my alarm I tend to feel far more lethargic and sapped of energy the rest of the day. There's nothing special about me—if I can train my mind to do this, so can you.

What's great about waking up early is you'll have at least a couple of hours all to yourself to do whatever you please! Most of the world hasn't woken up yet, there's a feeling of calm in the air, and you're surrounded by nothing but peacefulness. Journal, meditate, do some yoga, go for a run and watch the sunrise, write, work on your business, repeat your affirmations... the morning is *yours*, and you'll have no interruptions.

In addition, the morning is when our motivation is at its highest, and this steadily decreases throughout the day. By the time you finish work and get home, you're way less likely to go and work out, write a chapter of your book, or be doing your best thinking. You'll find yourself falling into the trap of saying, *"I'll do it tomorrow"*— and we all know how that can quickly become never. Whatever you want to spend more of your time doing or learning should begin in the morning.

You might find your current morning looks similar to this:

Alarm goes. Hit snooze. Wake up late. Jump in the shower and pull on any clean clothes you can find. No time for breakfast. Down some coffee for a quick energy boost. Rush to work.

Those are all simply bad habits that you've gradually incorporated into your morning, and now they've become your routine. The great news is any bad habit can be replaced with a new positive one in an average of two months (or 66 days)—sometimes sooner, sometimes later. Whether you want to cut down on the amount of junk food you consume, work out more, or find the time to pick up a new hobby, you just need to do it consecutively, and in time it will become second nature to you. The same goes for waking up early. You might tell me you're the polar opposite of a morning person and that you do your best work late at night, but wake up early consistently each morning (and get to bed earlier too!) and see if you feel any different.

And remember, it takes time to get used to a new routine and find your perfect rhythm, so don't be hard on yourself while you're figuring this out. Just do your best—that's all you can do.

Let the morning be whatever you desire it to be. Set it up right and this will have a positive domino effect on your entire day. All the things you've struggled to make time for will become possible, and you'll feel like you're achieving so much more each day—because you will be! Not only will this help you on the way to living a more fulfilled life, but you'll also feel centred and happier because you're finally giving your heart what it craves most.

Quit sabotaging yourself!

I can't *stand* the phrase "YOLO" (you only live once) and the way it's thrown around as an excuse to be utterly blasé about your life and the choices you make each day. What probably originated as an inspirational metaphor for living life to the fullest quickly became used as a get-out clause to do whatever the hell you want instead of what you know in your heart of hearts you *should* do.

What YOLO really means is you need to get real serious about this one life you've been blessed with because it's incredibly fragile and precious. Don't waste this *one* chance on being a shadow of the fierce and fabulous woman I know lives inside of you, waiting to be released.

Deep down, I *know* you don't think "living" means getting unconscious on alcohol, or staying in a relationship that is making you feel terribly lonely, or wishing Monday through Friday away so you can finally escape your job and have fun. I know you know better. I know you desire so much more than this half-lived life. If you know it and I know it, it's time to quit sabotaging yourself, girlfriend!

Give up the things in your life that you know aren't helping you grow and move forward—anything that's dimming your glow. This will make space for what you truly love and help you focus on your long-term plans and goals. You might think you'll be bored or living a life void of all fun and enjoyment because that's *exactly* what I first thought, but in fact the opposite reigns true.

You'll find yourself living a life overflowing with far more love, happiness, and fulfillment than you ever dreamed of before. It's time for you to step wholly into the beautiful new story you're creating, and be far too occupied by your zest, your fire, and your magic to ever look back again.

GLOW

GUIDE

How do you currently spend your free time?

Make a list of all the things you've always wanted to do, but never thought you have time for:
(e.g. writing a book, learning a new language, training for a marathon)

Think about what you could do less of in order to make time for these:

What does your dream daily routine look like?

If time wasn't holding you back, what would you do? Fill your day with all the things you love as well as all the things you've always wanted to do but never found time to. I love to include things that are focused on self-development and nourishing my soul.

<u>**Your mission:**</u> Plan out your day (include time slots and allow for your day job and other responsibilities), and implement it gradually. Tomorrow, pick one new thing to do, the following day add something else, and keep going until your day mirrors that of your dreams.

Download your free workbook at **shanijay.com/glowguide** and get the worksheet for this Glow Guide (plus a few extra gifts!), along with all the others in this book.

SHOW UP FOR YOURSELF

"I love to see a young girl go out and grab the world by the lapels. Life's a bitch. You've got to go out and kick ass."

— Maya Angelou

Back when I was working in the fashion industry, I'd wake up on a Sunday morning and that '*Smonday*' feeling (when it's Sunday and still technically the weekend, but you can't help but think about going to work tomorrow where all the bullshit and drama would start up again) would weigh heavily on my heart. I was still on my own time and I should have been relaxing and enjoying myself, but all I could think about was returning to my self-made prison in just a few hours.

Waking up Monday through Friday left me with a blue feeling inside as I knew I had to spend the majority of my day with people I couldn't *stand*, doing a job I'd completely fallen out of love with. Once I got there, throughout the day, I'd often have these strange feelings of being in a dream-like state and thinking, "*This is not my real life. I'm not supposed to be here.*" Sadly, it *was* my life and no matter how many times I pinched myself, I *was* there.

I knew if I didn't make some big changes I'd be stuck in this place void of all happiness forever. I knew this life would never be enough for me, and I wasn't content with being someone who didn't at least *try* to turn things around. I couldn't accept that this was all there was. In my heart, I felt like something was majorly disconnected and it was up to me to start aligning my life with what lit me up and what made me excited to face the day each morning.

Up until then, I'd merely been accepting my circumstances and trying to convince myself that I was happy and in the grand scheme of things I'd been dealt a pretty good hand—but those are just lies we tell ourselves to make it through the day. I wasn't being the best person I knew I had the capacity to be, and I was ready to start showing up for myself in bold and beautiful ways.

Fall in love with the process, not the result

You can learn, have, or be anything you desire in this life as long as you want it enough. You could become a kinder, more loving person to your family and friends. You could train to climb Mount Everest. You could write a best-selling novel. You could become a millionaire. You could find the partner you've been searching for your whole life. You could start a thriving business with your greatest passion. You could be happy, fulfilled, and excited to bounce out of your cosy bed each morning. The woman you *know* you can be awaits you on the other side of the climb.

But you've got to commit yourself to the *process* of transforming your life, instead of just the end result. If you merely want what awaits you at the end and you don't respect the lengthy process it takes to arrive there, then you're likely to give up long before you make it. Learn to fall in love with the process of turning your life around and becoming your best self. Fill the process with all that lights you up because when you love what you're doing each day, you'll want to keep doing more of it.

The process promises to be tough, but it's possible, and I know you've got the stamina and courage it takes to show up for yourself each and every day and keep going no matter what. Breaking down your dreams and desires into smaller, attainable goals that don't intimidate you or feel out of reach will be the vital stepping stones you need along the way to a beautiful, joy-filled life.

It's like eating a slice of cake—you wouldn't try and wedge a whole slice into your mouth in one go, would you? No, you'll devour it one forkful at a time, which is much easier and also makes it far more delicious and satisfying. That might seem like a ridiculous analogy, but I love cake (who doesn't?) and those same principles apply to any challenge you'll ever face!

Think of all those times you've begun the day by looking at your endless to-do list and felt de-motivated before you'd even started. When you focus on the end goal too much, it can throw you off track and stop you from making progress. That's such an exhausting and completely unnecessary way to navigate your life.

I set myself two or three BIG goals each year at the very start that I want to achieve during the next 12 months, followed by three to five smaller goals at the beginning of each month that are all working towards those larger goals—the key here is I only ever work on *one* goal at a time.

Focusing on one goal at a time will help your dreams to feel within reach and far more manageable too. Begin with the very first step you need to take to get started, and be sure to keep building on this with each new goal you set. The smaller goals on the way to your big ones should become progressively more challenging and bring you out of your comfort zone.

Setting new goals regularly is important because they help you to continue improving and challenging yourself to be better each day, and they also help to keep you motivated throughout the process. Make sure you stop to celebrate each and every one along the way—a glass of something pink and sparkling is optional, but strongly suggested!

Think of your life goals as your North Star—they will always be there twinkling in the skies above to guide you to where you want to go, but ultimately it's up to *you* to take the path that leads you there and stay on track.

It all comes down to this: Are you willing to learn to love and commit to the process for the chance at living the life you've always dreamed of?

Nothing worth having will be easy

It's gonna be damn hard work because if it wasn't, everyone around you would be floating on cloud nine and living out their dreams. But they're not. Stop and look at them next time, the sea of people around you every day. They're always in a rush, they're not paying any attention to their surroundings, they're attempting to do multiple things at once, they're not present in any of their moments... life is slowly passing them by and they're too preoccupied with the stress and pain of their everyday routine to even notice.

You have to decide that you are worth the grind, sweat, and tears that come with making huge changes in your life and stepping far outside of your comfort zone. And let me tell you now, you *are* worth it.

Those overnight success stories you often hear about are all actually super summarised versions of five, ten, even twenty-year stories. There is no such thing as an *overnight* success. Success is the product of years of hard work, patience, picking yourself back up when things don't work out, and never, *ever* giving up. Most people don't even start or they quit halfway when things get a little tough.

Who will you choose to be?

I need you to know that you have just as much of a chance at living your dreams as anybody else does in this world. Really, you do. Believe that. Be brave enough to choose your own path, commit to travelling all the way down it, and I promise you'll find your way to some amazing things. Challenges, experiences, and accomplishments you never knew you would face, let alone conquer.

Something you've created solely from your heart and hands. Adventures through exotic lands. The freedom to live your life as you please. Double rainbows. Changing someone's life. Making more money than you ever thought possible. A real kind of honest and true love, like you only read about in fairy tales. More laughter, more sunshine, more glitter in your veins. An extraordinary life you can say you *chose*, you didn't merely settle for.

Today can be the beginning of it all—you must simply decide that it *will* be.

Be sure to bet on you. Back yourself, and head down the road that you know you want and need to take. Because we only get one shot at this crazy thing called life. No going back, no do-overs, and no second chances.

Just do it!

You have just as much of a shot at being successful as anybody else does. Maybe you're not lucky enough to be born rich, and maybe you aren't as smart or as skilled as you believe other people are, but you know what? That's not an excuse. Plenty of people are born with next to nothing, and they work their butts off to make a success of their life. They don't allow anything or anyone to hold them back from the person they want to be, and neither should you.

There are no excuses. Get smart. Learn from those people you admire. Read books. Take an online course. Get a mentor. Don't know how to do something? Google it. We are all so fortunate to be born in a time when everything can be found at our fingertips.

It all comes down to hard work, and no one can do the work for you—that's 100% on you. You can enlist help from people along the way, but the real effort has to come from you. Show up for yourself every single day and put in the hours. Show yourself you're worth the effort because you *are*. Keep focused on your why and take one day at a time. Don't allow yourself to get overwhelmed and disheartened by looking at how far you've still got left to go. Think of all you can do each day to move *one* step closer towards your higher self. She's rooting for you just as much as I am—we all want to see the beauty of your true colours illuminating the world.

What's sad is, most people *aren't* willing to show up for themselves every single day. They allow themselves to become distracted, thrown off course, or demotivated at the first few hurdles and end up giving up before they've even been tested. Because let's be honest, it's far easier to live a cushy life where you're not pushing yourself to your limits. It's far easier to get home after a long day at work and eat a pizza instead of hitting the gym. It's easier to stay in bed a little longer instead of waking up and getting started on that business plan. Of course it is. But an easy life is a life half-lived, and you were always destined for so much more.

The only person who will ever be standing in the way of the woman you desire to be is *you*. Commit to the process, show up and do the work each day, and you'll surprise yourself with how different you feel within and the better choices you naturally start to make.

Who you're going to be is still very much up to you.

Always do your best

But remember your best will vary all the time. When you wake up first thing in the morning after a peaceful night's sleep, you'll feel more energised and zippy than you will when you're lethargic right before you go to bed at night. Your mood, whether happy or sad, will effect your best. Being sober as opposed to drunk and eating clean instead of eating junk food will affect it too. Not to say you shouldn't indulge in a bar of chocolate, just be aware of how everything you consume (physically and mentally) will affect you. Sometimes you'll be able to give more, and sometimes you'll have to be content with giving a little less.

Over time, the more you practice doing your best, the better it will become—this is how you can continue to raise the bar of success for yourself. Don't push yourself to do more or make excuses for doing less than your best, and try not to judge yourself through the process. Do your best because you *want* to, not because you have to.

As long as you do your best, that will always be enough. The world isn't looking for a superwoman who has been gifted special powers—you as you are right now is all it takes. The you right now is more than enough. Everything you'll ever need can be found within.

GLOW

GUIDE

Goal setting for glow getters

Without goals, you'll lack focus and direction, and the *way* you set them will have an impact on the likelihood of you achieving them.

Here are the 10 golden rules when it comes to goal setting:

1. **Brainstorm** - Make a list of all the wonderful things you'd like to do in your life, anything that sounds fun and lights you up when you think of it, and then choose the ones that stand out most to you from the list.

2. **Find your WHY** - As you already know, getting clear on why you want to achieve your goals is powerful because it will help provide purpose, clarity, and all the motivation you need to see it through to the end.

3. **Pick ONE goal to focus on at a time** - It's hard to focus on more than one goal at a time, and it is also likely to overwhelm you. Having one thing to focus on means you can throw all of your energy into making it happen.

4. **Write it down** - Writing anything down signifies you stating your intention and putting things in motion. It also helps to have your goal somewhere you can see it every day and be reminded of what you're working towards.

5. **Break it down into steps** - Define the very last thing you'll need to do in order to achieve your goal, then the step before

that, and the step before that one, and keep going until you get to the very first step you need to take in getting started.

6. **Set yourself a timeline** - Set a "by when" date for your goal—when you want to achieve it by—as well as dates for all the mini-steps too.

7. **Find someone to hold you accountable** - It's hard keeping yourself motivated all the way on your journey, and it can really help to have a friend, mentor, or coach to hold you accountable to your goals and even provide feedback along the way. As soon as you tell someone about your plans, they become real.

8. **Take action on that first step TODAY** - Whatever that very first step on your goal breakdown was, start on it today. Don't put things off—commit to this journey *today*. The sooner you start, the sooner you'll get there!

9. **Review them frequently** - It's up to you how often you review your goals (daily, weekly, or monthly), but make sure they inspire and populate your daily to-do lists. Every time you review your goal, look at how far you've come and think about the next step you need to take to move forward.

10. **Keep going** - Don't allow yourself to forget your goal or be distracted from it. Always keep it in sight, remain focused, and put all your energy into achieving what you set out to. You'll thank yourself when you finally get there.

Tick-box trick

Every time I've been working on a new project or big challenge, I've found the tick-box method to be incredibly effective in keeping my motivation levels high and pushing me forward, even when I'm feeling sluggish.

<u>Your mission:</u> Draw up a simple table with a series of equal-sized boxes to represent the number of days you want to continue a new habit or work towards a specific goal (e.g. going for a run, writing in your journal, eating clean). Each day you successfully complete your task, you get to put a big tick in the box, and if you don't manage to stick to it, you have to leave the box blank.

I find this simple exercise helps to keep you on track because it's human nature to want to see a full page of ticks—we like winning!

Print out your very own goal guidebook and ready-made tick sheet for free at **shanijay.com/glowguide**, and get all the other worksheets from this book too!

FIND YOUR TRIBE

"I want to be around people that do things. I don't want to be around people anymore that judge or talk about what people do. I want to be around people who dream, and support, and do things... Find a group of people who challenge and inspire you; spend a lot of time with them, and it will change your life."

— Amy Poehler

Every woman needs at least one soul sister in her life who champions her on her journey, celebrates with her when she wins, and consoles her when she falls down. The path you're on is hard enough as it is, so it's imperative you have the right people around you, supporting you along the way. Naturally, you will encounter people who don't have your back and simply don't *get* it. Be strong enough to continue down your path, even if the world is telling you to go in a different direction.

This is how you'll find your *tribe*.

Dealing with lack of support from family and friends

You've gotta remember, you are on a path to transform your life. That's a *big* deal. Most people will never commit to such a huge upheaval because it's extremely tough, it's messy, and at times painful. The journey you're on right now will force you to make many difficult choices along the way, and you have to decide that the woman you're aspiring to become is worth it. You have to choose her over *everything*.

Not everyone is going to understand what you're doing. The people you thought loved and supported you the most and the people who have been in your life the longest might not comprehend or even like the positive changes you're making. While your family might continue to love and care for you unconditionally, they probably can't fully appreciate what you're going through, and therefore they won't be able to support you in the way you wish they would.

The same goes for partners and friends. Just a few years ago you might've had everything in common, but now that your priorities and desires have altered, you might find that you're both naturally drifting further and further apart. And while it's sad, you've got to know that it's normal to grow apart from people. It's normal to fall out of love with someone or to move into a completely different friendship circle, and you should never allow the fear of making new friendships and relationships hold you back in ones that no longer align with who you are. Because there's no guarantee when it comes to anyone or *anything* in this life. We all grow and change as people, and that's okay. It's okay to be selfish sometimes and think of *your* needs instead of everybody else's. You're allowed to leave. You're allowed to move on.

You might also find that not everyone in your life will be happy seeing you thrive and transform into this fabulous, confident glow getter. They might want to selfishly keep you down at their level, and they might be jealous of your success and accomplishments. Some prefer to be surrounded with people they view as weaker in order to inflate themselves. Again, this is just a normal part of life you'll experience sooner or later. It's hard to ever truly know someone or know what their real motives are in regards to being a part of your life.

Since reaching my twenties, before I even thought about switching careers, I began to ruthlessly cut people out of my life who I know aren't bringing anything positive into it. That might sound harsh, but the truth is there's no point in maintaining a friendship or relationship that isn't serving you. Now, don't get me wrong—I *don't* mean you should make friends with people merely because of what they can do for you, but a relationship is a two-way street. It's give and take. You should both be benefitting from that relationship and becoming better people because of it.

I'm a firm believer that people always come into our lives for a reason—they're either a blessing or a lesson, and not everyone is supposed to stick around for the long haul. Sometimes you have to part ways with people you've known a long time. This is all part of the growing process. It's okay to let go and move on. In fact, it's imperative that we do because in doing so we make room for new people to walk into our life who are aligned with the woman we're striving to be.

If you lose someone but find *yourself* in the process, you won. So don't worry about losing people around you along the way. If someone is meant to be in your life, you won't have to think twice about it—you'll know.

> "The people making you feel guilty for going your own way and choosing your own life are simply saying, 'Look at me. I'm better than you because my chains are bigger.' It takes courage to break those chains and define your own life." — Psalm Isadora

It sucks when the people you love aren't supportive of you, especially when you know you'd be there for them and happy for them no matter what. Trust me, I know. I've been there many times and I *get* it. But that's just life—not everyone will be like you. You have to find the strength and the courage within to keep on going and remind yourself of the bigger picture.

The older you get, the more you begin to realise the only person in this world who can ever be guaranteed to have your back is you. You might find yourself standing on your own more times than you'd like, but get comfortable standing there. Get comfortable with who you are and what your heart wants. You might be somebody's employee, somebody's best friend, or somebody's daughter, but first and foremost, you are *you*.

You might be lucky enough to have a number of people in your life who love you, but the love you have for yourself should always be your lifeline. If everybody around you disappeared, would your love be enough for you to carry on?

The answer should always be yes.

When there's no one to share your journey with

When you're in the midst of changing your life, it will often be uncomfortable or painful. You'll need a constant source of inspiration and motivation to keep pushing forward, and now is the most crucial time to have a strong inner circle of good people around you who you can truly rely on to support you on your way. But life doesn't always work out that way and you might find yourself alone.

You can begin to feel isolated and struggle to navigate your way through the dark without any inkling of light to offer you a sense of direction and hope. So many obstacles will be scattered along your path and our natural human instinct is to turn to someone we love for support, comfort, and guidance.

The simple act of sharing how we're feeling (with anyone) can help to relieve us of some of the pent-up stress and anxiety that might be overwhelming us, but we're always more inclined to share those feelings with someone who's going to understand and be able to offer us some tangible advice that is rooted in their own past experiences. It's natural for us to seek out those who have already been there and are more likely to empathise with our struggles because they can help us to figure them out as quickly and painlessly as possible.

I've found one of the hardest parts about this process is not having anyone to share your journey with because chances are the people in your life have never been through what you're currently experiencing. They've never pushed themselves to their limits. They've never truly chased after their dreams. They've never gone through anything quite as transformative and life-changing as what you're going through right now. That in itself can be the initial disconnect in you beginning to drift apart from the people in your life and forming new relationships with others who are on a similar wavelength to you.

When it comes down to it, no one wants to be in a friendship or a romantic partnership where they feel like they're not understood.

We want to be surrounded with people who are vibrating on the same level as we are. We want to feel aligned with the desires and values of those whom we spend our precious time with. We want to find our *tribe*.

Regardless of who might come in or out of your life during this time, you've got to remain focused on your goals and your mission. Remind yourself again of what it will mean to you to succeed in changing your current circumstances. You have chosen this path, and it's a different one to what most people choose.

Why you need a support system of like-minded soul sisters and where to find them

I'm confident that even if you found yourself completely deserted, you'd be able to look inside and discover the strength to power on through the darkness and survive all the way to the other side. You're a fierce and fabulous warrior, and I believe in your power. But why struggle alone if you don't have to?

Even if you know you've got this all on your own, it can help tremendously to have just *one* person in your life who you can turn to, who you can share all of your highs and lows with. Someone who can help make your life a little simpler or less stressful. Let's be honest, life is already real messy at the best of times—you don't need to be making it harder than it already is!

What you need is a soul sister, or a tribe of soul sisters, who have got your back through it all. Someone who shares your way of thinking, understands who you are, and is a positive source of energy in your life. Someone who is honest and holds you accountable to your goals and dreams. Someone who lifts you up, inspires you to be better every day, and wants to see you succeed. Someone who's not gonna do the hard work for you, but will offer their support and guidance when you're in need. None of the usual gossipping, bitching, or cattiness which tends to present itself in a lot of female relationships—leave that bullshit behind because it doesn't serve anyone.

You'll instantly know when you find her. There should be a natural, constant flow of good energy zipping back and forth, where you're on the same level and vibing off each other. When you're together, you should have that intuitive feeling deep down in the pit of your stomach that this is *right* and feels good. Otherwise, what's the damn point?

The best friendships develop over time. Unfortunately, you can't simply wish for a soul sister and have her appear overnight. So the best place to start is by meeting and connecting with as many women as possible. Think of it as being similar to the dating game—the more dates you go on, the more likely you are to stumble upon a good one instead of another slimy frog masquerading as Prince Charming. It's a no-brainer. You've gotta put yourself out there and be proactive. If you want something you've never had before, you've gotta do something you've never *done* before.

So where can you hope to find a like-minded soul sister?

Online is the perfect place to start. It's fairly casual, the relationship can grow at a pace that's comfortable for you, and there are options to video chat or even meet up face to face if you want to turn a URL friendship to IRL.

Shortly after deciding I needed to escape my 9-5, I knew I had to force myself to start thinking on a much higher level than I currently was, and surrounding myself with women who were already on that level seemed like a great way to help me up my game. So I started searching for groups on social networks that I already hung out on, I started building real relationships with like-minded women I didn't know, and I looked for mentor groups and local networking events for writers and entrepreneurs. Whatever you're trying to accomplish or succeed at, I guarantee there's someone else in the world trying to do the same thing. Have a look and see.

Once I found a suitable group or page, I put myself out there, got involved in conversations, and took a chance by messaging certain women who I felt I had an initial connection with. Of course, not all of those interactions led somewhere and that's to be expected.

One of the best things about the online world is it doesn't matter if you're shy or introverted because you're not on the spot like you are when speaking to someone in real life. You can pause before you reply to a message, you can delete things and re-type—there's no pressure. And you can literally connect with women on the other side of the world—it's incredible when you think about it.

Allow yourself to be *open* to a real friendship, and it might just blossom somewhere you least expect it to. I've been lucky enough to connect with some incredibly inspiring women over the past year from my hometown of the UK as well as in the U.S., Europe, South Africa, India, the Phillipines, and Australia too. Women who understand and support my mission, women who are out there making fabulous things happen for themselves, and women who are clued in on the importance and value of women empowering other women—because when we do *amazing* things start to happen.

The Glow Getter Tribe

There's already so much stacked against us simply for being born as women today. We've made great progress, but in certain countries we still have no rights and are treated as second-class citizens, while many men believe we are born to merely satisfy their needs. The last thing we need is to be turning on each *other*. We need to come *together* and start using that all-powerful force of sisterhood to lift each other up. We are all so much stronger when we rise together.

Like a lot of people, in my early teens I was bullied at school which made me feel like I didn't *belong*. It was a classic case of girl-on-girl crime—girls being extremely bitchy and spiteful and putting others down in order to make themselves feel better. Bullies are often the most miserable and lonely of people; they just disguise it well, and they feed off the weakness in others in order to feel more powerful and in control. Those early years hugely knocked my confidence and damaged my self-worth, and it took me the best part of 10 years to build that back up again and regain my strength. It also made it difficult for me to trust women after that, and I thought if this is what all women are like, finding a group of sisters is *not* worth the hassle.

I'm painfully aware that I'm not the only woman who has experienced this and I certainly won't be the last. There are so many women who *still* struggle with their self-worth today because of past events. With this weighing heavily on my heart, in mid-2016, I launched a self-love and kindness movement, The Glow Getter Tribe, from my bedroom, which aims to help women realise and celebrate their awesomeness. It's about women uniting together, learning to feel good about themselves inside and out, and recognising that they have their very own sparkle inside just waiting to dazzle the world. When we focus on love, positive energy, and sisterhood, we subconsciously invite more of it into our lives.

Sometimes, all we need is someone else letting us know they *believe* in us, that we *are* special, and that things aren't ever as bad as they may seem on the surface. The people we surround ourselves with will have a greater impact on us than we can even begin to imagine, so we must choose those people wisely.

Your tribe of soul sisters will be the ones who you can laugh with, bawl your eyes out with, share your experiences with, and figure out how to overcome your challenges with. They will be standing loyally and lovingly by your side through it all, when you're just getting started, to proudly watching you blossom into the woman you always said you were going to be.

GLOW

GUIDE

#GLOWGETTERTRIBE

Who in your life is currently not supportive of your transformation journey?

How do you feel when you're with them?

How would you like to feel instead?

What are the qualities you're looking for in a soul sister?
(Support, mentorship, positive energy, kindness, etc.)

Places you can connect with like-minded women:

- ❤ Facebook groups
- ❤ Instagram
- ❤ Local networking events
- ❤ Mentor sites
- ❤ Female-orientated support groups (business and general ones)

Get some GLOW

The Glow Getter Tribe was created for women who want to attract more love and happiness into their lives, build their self-confidence, and realise their worth.

It's free to join, and as soon as you do, you'll be sent a free 7-day self-love challenge where you'll learn:

- ❤ How to bring positive vibes into your life
- ❤ How to change the way you see yourself
- ❤ Your own Goddess ritual
- ❤ How to practice gratitude and feel more thankful
- ❤ To love who you are, from the inside out
- ❤ A clear sense of self-worth
- ❤ And most importantly—that you are *enough*.

You'll also get weekly Love Letters from me filled with inspiration, kindness, and a generous sprinkle of sparkle!

Relax, grab a glass of pink, come on in, and join our tribe over at **shanijay.com/glowgetter**.

IT'S ALWAYS DARKEST
BEFORE THE DAWN

"I think women are scared of feeling powerful and strong and brave sometimes. There's nothing wrong with being afraid. It's not the absence of fear, it's overcoming it and sometimes you just have to blast through and have faith."

— Emma Watson

Life has a funny way of pushing us to our very limits. From the outset, it might *seem* as though the universe is conspiring against you and doing everything in its power to make you give up, but what it's *really* doing is pushing you a little bit further each day to make you stronger, smarter, and wiser. It's finding out whether you're serious or not about changing your life. All of the inevitable obstacles and setbacks you will face are merely the universe's way of daring you to keep going.

Just keep going. You will find your light, and it will guide you through the darkness.

Face your fears

I think a lot of us confuse being fearless with having no fears. The reality is it's totally normal to be afraid of certain things. There's nothing wrong with being afraid—it doesn't mean you're any less strong or powerful because of it. Not a single soul on this planet is fearless. We all have our own internal demons: things that make us feel anxious, stressed, or scared. Some of us are just better at masking those fears than others. Even when we find the courage to face those fears, they will naturally be replaced with new ones.

> *"To me, Fearless is not the absence of fear. It's not being completely unafraid. To me, Fearless is having fears. Fearless is having doubts. Lots of them. To me, Fearless is living in spite of those things that scare you to death."*
> — *Taylor Swift*

You know what being fearless *really* means?

Fearless is leaving a toxic relationship even when you're scared of being alone.

Fearless is quitting your job because it's sapping the joy from your life, even when you don't yet have another job lined up.

Fearless is doing the right thing and standing up for someone else who is unable to find their voice, even when nobody is standing with you.

Fearless is deciding to look inside yourself and muster the strength to always face those fears, no matter how much they cripple you within. No matter how long it takes. No matter how many times you don't succeed. No matter how uncomfortable or painful it might feel in the moment.

We're all plagued with our own fears, but it's how we choose to *deal* with those fears that ultimately shapes who we will be and what we can achieve—and it is a choice. Ask yourself, what's the worst thing that could happen if you decide to confront your biggest fear today? What you've conjured in your imagination is probably ten times worse than anything that is even remotely likely to happen. We're all such *drama queens* in that way—me included.

What I'm slowly discovering is the importance of getting comfortable with feeling *uncomfortable*. The importance of stepping outside of our safe and cosy comfort zones. Because we already know what we know. It's easy. It's comfortable. It's unchallenging. And so it doesn't do anything to help us grow further. The way I see it is if you're not growing, you're only dying.

What do you have to lose by throwing yourself into something new? Something you have no idea how to do? Something that terrifies you to your bones as you think about it just now?

At first you'll be afraid. You might feel scared or anxious and those voices in the back of your head will probably tell you you're a fool for even *attempting* to do this. Acknowledge the presence of those feelings and voices. Allow them to enter your mind and then just sit with them for a while. Get comfortable being uncomfortable because this is a powerful feeling. It helps you to break down those barriers and negative thought processes you have ingrained in your mind.

Sitting with feelings of fear and uncertainty will help you push through to the other side with the realisation that these are merely just *thoughts*. They aren't real, and they will come and go. Any fear you feel inside is simply your imagination running wild. The more you practice this, the easier it will become to take on bigger challenges and be even bolder in the way you confront all of your future worries and fears.

Be fearless by embracing your deepest and darkest fears every day. Never allow them to hold you back from living your best life. Remember, what you hide from only keeps you small. Face your fears *today* and watch how you manage to achieve and conquer things you never dreamed you could.

Don't quit when the going gets tough

This is the point along your journey where the majority of people are most likely to give up. They're not seeing results fast enough, their new way of life feels too alien and difficult to adhere to, and they can't see a glimmer of light in sight ahead. So they decide they're not going to carry on, and they comfortably slip back into their old routines and habits.

What you don't realise is by this point you're so much closer to your end goal than you *think* you are. You've already put in so much time and hard work, and that woman you've always dreamed of being looms just upon the horizon. She is within reach. Whatever you do, don't stop now.

It can be testing when you look around (especially when you're "harmlessly" scrolling through social media) and all you can see are people who seem to have this life thing figured out. People travelling the world doing all kinds of exciting things, others who have found their soul mates, and let's not forget those teenage YouTube stars who are earning a sizeable living from filming themselves doing their hair and makeup in their bedroom. You might find yourself wondering, *how come they've got things all figured out and my life is a total shit show?*

Well, the reality is they probably worked hard to get where they are right now, and even if they didn't, *nobody's* life is perfect. We've all got our own baggage that we're dealing with quietly behind the scenes, so it's important to maintain perspective at all times. Ankati Day shared these incredibly powerful words below which puts our journeys into total perspective:

> "At age 23, Oprah was fired from her first reporting job.
> At age 24, Stephen King was working as a janitor and living in a trailer.
> At age 27, Vincent Van Gogh failed as a missionary and decided to go to art school.
> At age 28, J.K. Rowling was a suicidal single parent living on welfare.
> At age 30, Martha Stewart was a stockbroker.
> Julia Child released her first cookbook at age 39, and got her own cooking show at age 51.
> Vera Wang failed to make the Olympic figure skating team, didn't get the Editor-in-Chief position at Vogue, and designed her first dress at age 40.
> Alan Rickman gave up his graphic design career to pursue acting at age 42.
> Samuel L. Jackson didn't get his first movie role until he was 46.
> Morgan Freeman landed his first MAJOR movie role at age 52.
> Kathryn Bigelow only reached international success when she made The Hurt Locker at age 57.
> Louise Bourgeois didn't become a famous artist until she

was 78.

Whatever your dream is, it is not too late to achieve it. You aren't a failure because you haven't found fame and fortune by the age of 21. Hell, it's okay if you don't even know what your dream is yet. Even if you're flipping burgers, waiting tables or answering phones today, you never know where you'll end up tomorrow.

Never tell yourself you're too old to make it.
Never tell yourself you missed your chance.
Never tell yourself that you aren't good enough.
You can do it. Whatever it is."

Just imagine what would've happened if any of those people had given up before they witnessed their dreams transform into reality? What if they had decided it was too late? What if they had allowed failure to discourage them?

It's true what they say, it's always darkest before the dawn. Your most painful moments and experiences will always be on the cusp of a major breakthrough—you just have to find the strength within to *keep going*. Those moments where you feel like giving up or you feel like you're not strong enough to pull yourself through this, are all a significant part of your journey in reaching your higher self. They are testing you, and it's on you to not only rise to the occasion, but show yourself who's boss while you're there!

An obstacle is how you choose to see it

On the surface, an obstacle might appear as a setback or something keeping you from your dream life, but the truth about obstacles is they're neither good nor bad, but all rooted in how you decide to look at them. Obstacles can actually help to push you forward on your way to where you need to go.

What feels like struggle and frustration is often development and growth. What looks like failure is often actually the beginning of success. Overcoming an obstacle is simply a way of declaring to the universe that you're worthy of more. Once it believes you can take it, more will come your way.

Transformation is, by definition, going through a dramatic change. You're attempting to alter *years* of habits that have built up, vast experiences that have shaped you, and internal thought processes that are one with your mind. There will be growing pains all along the way. But without those hard times and those tough lessons, you wouldn't be the woman you already are *today*.

Think about everything that has happened to you so far in your life. Whether you acknowledged it as good or bad, it has either slightly or significantly shaped your character, your heart, and your soul. You probably wish you could hit pass on all those lessons life has thrown your way and fast forward through the pain because sometimes it's simply unbearable. I empathise with where you're coming from, but if you did that, you wouldn't be sitting where you are today with the certainty that you have the inner strength to pull yourself through *anything*.

You wouldn't have half the courage, knowledge, or wisdom that you find deep within yourself today. You wouldn't be the strong woman that others have come to know and love. So don't ever wish your hard times away. Don't sit there feeling sorry for yourself, and don't think that any scars you've collected have had a negative impact on you. That pain and those hardships shaped you into the strong woman you were always meant to *be*.

Dealing with stress

In the modern world, the majority of us are overworking ourselves and not taking the necessary time to unplug and recharge, allowing stress to swoop in unnoticed and takeover. In the West, we live in a culture where we (absurdly) think it's *good* to be busy all the time, pile tasks onto our daily to-do lists, and skip on regular breaks because we've got far too much to be getting on with.

Leaving work aside, imagine trying to transform your life on top of this everyday pressure. There's a good chance you might end up feeling overwhelmed and totally stressed out, so I want to take some time to explore what stress is and how you can best deal with it if it does arise.

Stress is usually a state of mental or emotional strain, resulting from adverse or demanding circumstances that you're not used to. When you're stressed, your body feels like it's under attack and goes into "fight or flight" mode, and may leave you unable to think straight or concentrate. This can have a huge impact on your home and work life, as well as your health.

Fight mode - You feel agitated and can become aggressive towards others, which can harm our relationships and give us a negative reputation.

Flight mode - Instead of facing your stressor head on, you remove yourself from the situation and avoid it, which can lead to it escalating and increasing our stress levels.

It's important to remember that being stressed is different than having a bad day. We all experience our share of bad days, but prolonged stress is what you need to look out for.

How you decide to tackle it will play a significant role in either helping yourself or magnifying your problems.

Negative ways to deal with stress: Drinking excessive amounts of caffeine or alcohol, smoking cigarettes, isolating yourself from others, sleeping too little or too much, binging on comfort food, burying your head in the sand and ignoring your problems, and procrastinating.

The great news is there are many ways to deal with stress that don't involve scoffing a pint of Ben & Jerry's or chugging an entire bottle of wine!

Positive ways to deal with stress:

- ♥ Be sure to get a good night's sleep.
- ♥ Practice meditation or deep breathing.

- ♥ Stay hydrated throughout the day.

- ♥ Eat a healthy balanced diet (and make sure you're not skipping any meals).

- ♥ Exercise daily.

- ♥ Unplug yourself from technology as often as you can.

- ♥ Start thinking positively.

- ♥ Practice gratitude.

- ♥ Get organised and more efficient with your time.

- ♥ Learn to say *no*.

Make sure you're helping yourself and dealing with stress as soon as it begins to set in. The earlier you address it, the easier it will be to combat.

Remember, this journey you're on is supposed to be *enjoyable*. Of course it's going to be tough along the way, but it's not supposed to be harmful or toxic. Stress is something that affects the majority of us at some point in our lives to different degrees, and that's to be expected. Especially when you're forcing yourself to do things that are way out of your comfort zone while still expecting the very best from yourself. That's never going to be plain sailing, but if it was would it be half as rewarding when you finally get there? Probably not. Half of the satisfaction lies in overcoming all of your struggles along the way and being able to look back proudly at just how far you've come.

I like to think maybe it's not always stress that we're experiencing, despite thinking so—perhaps it's real growth. It's dealing with being uncomfortable. It's fighting against the old you and becoming a much stronger woman in the process.

How to stay motivated

One of the hardest parts about transforming your life is staying motivated. It's easy to start—anyone can start—but very few will remain consistent and see it through to the end.

I know I'm starting to sound like a broken record at this point, but you've always got to think back to your initial *why*. You'll find a great source of reassurance, inspiration, and motivation in the deep reasoning behind *why* you want to change your life. Whether it's because you want to be a better partner or parent, you want to feel healthier and happier, or you want more freedom—or even all of the above—continue to ask yourself why.

Another idea that works extremely well for many people is finding yourself an accountabilibuddy—someone to hold you accountable to what you say you're going to do. This can be a total stranger you connect with online or one of your closest soul sisters; the important thing is you *must* be able to count on them to do their job and hold you accountable. It helps to find someone who's going through the same transformation as you, or has already come out the other side, because they'll have more of an understanding of your situation, but it's not necessary.

An accountabilibuddy is someone you touch bases with each week and tell them a specific goal you're going to achieve in the next week or month. They will do the same and then you'll connect the following week to see if you've both met your goals. The idea is that once you tell someone your plans they become *real*, and it puts you under a little bit of positive pressure which means you're more likely to act because you don't want to have to tell someone you *didn't* do what you said you would.

You can even up the stakes by both putting a "punishment" in place if you don't meet your goals, like a small (but significant enough) wager. You'd be amazed at how much more effort you'll exert when there's something on the line!

Remind yourself often—I'm talking *daily*—of how far you've already come on this journey. Think back to who you were when you first began and who you are now because I promise you will have already gone through some incredible changes and grown in so many ways that might not have even crossed your mind. It's vital you *celebrate* all of your wins, no matter how big or small, along the way. Stop focusing on all of the things you've still gotta do, and start thinking about what you've done for a change.

One of the best tips I received from Kat Gaskin—founder of *Salty Pineapple* and total Queen—is to create a "WINS" folder on your laptop or phone, which I decided to turn into a physical pinboard because I'm one of those old-fashioned girls who always prefer to have something real instead of digital!

Anytime you have even the smallest of victories, you screenshot and save it, or you can print it out or write it down and pin it up. In time, you'll have an amazing collection of accomplishments staring back at you that are entirely of your own making, and what better motivation is there to keep pushing forward than *that*? We should be celebrating it *all*. Ending relationships with assholes. Good hair days. Choosing a green smoothie instead of a chocolate milkshake. Sticking with a new habit for a week. Getting promoted. Making someone else smile. Achieving our biggest goals. Starting a new job. Taking your bra off at the end of a tough day. Creating something fabulous from nothing. Letting go of a dream that doesn't align with us anymore... we should be celebrating *all* of it along the way.

Anytime I'm feeling a little low or deflated, I make sure I take a look at my past WINS and allow myself to feel good about everything I've achieved so far. It's a beautiful and much-needed reminder you're doing better than you *think* you are, and that you hold the key within yourself to the life you've always dreamed of living. Everything on this board exists, and it exists because of *you*. Nothing is out of reach and no dream is too big.

GLOW

GUIDE

Facing fears—the "what if" technique

To get over your fears, first you have to confront them.

Your mission:

1. **Write down your deepest** fears (one by one). Next, list the worst possible outcomes that could happen if you faced your fear, what you could do to prevent each of these from happening, and then what you could do to solve these hypothetical problems if they *did* happen.

2. **Write down all the potential benefits** you can imagine of trying or succeeding to overcome your fear.

3. **Ask yourself the cost of burying these fears** and doing nothing. If you were to continue to avoid this fear and allow it to influence your future decisions, what will your life look like in six months' time, one year, or even three years?

   Go deep with this one, and think about the ramifications emotionally, physically, financially, and spiritually too.

Doing this regularly will help you to evaluate and rationalise your fears, as well as take action towards overcoming them.

My deepest fears...

Celebrate your wins!

If you want to do this digitally, create a new folder or find an app like Evernote where you can write down and save screenshots of all of your accomplishments. You might decide to organise this by month, so you have a clearer picture of your progress.

If you want to create a physical WIN-board, get yourself a cork board or a large sheet of cardboard—anything that has enough space for you to pin all your future achievements on. Use this as rocket fuel for whenever you're feeling down or in need of a little confidence boost. Always cheer yourself on, glow getter!

Start writing done lists

I always need a to-do list to keep me on track for the day, but the trouble is we tend to overload ourselves with multiple tasks and then feel overwhelmed before we even get going. I try to have just *one* main priority each day and two to three smaller tasks that are less important.

At the end of the day, instead of berating myself for what I haven't done, I always make a point of writing down everything I *have* accomplished in that day—you can do this in your journal or in a separate notebook. It's a wonderful feeling listing all of the things you've achieved, and more often than not, you'll read it back to yourself and realise you had an awesome day filled with plenty of success! That in itself is great motivation to spur you on and keep you feeling positive and energised on your journey.

You can also head over to **shanijay.com/glowguide** and download your free workbook that includes a full worksheet for this chapter's Glow Guide, along with all the other chapters too!

HATERS GONNA HATE

"I am a woman with thoughts and questions and shit to say. I say if I'm beautiful. I say if I'm strong. You will not determine my story—I will."

— Amy Schumer

There are two types of people in this world:

1. The people who get off their butts and make things happen.

2. The people who sit around *watching* those people make things happen, wishing they could do the same, but are too lazy or lack the courage to get off their butts.

The fact that you're even reading this book (and you've gotten this far) tells me that you are the first type. The trouble with the second type of people is they wish their lives were better, but they're not willing to do anything about it, so they're often jealous or resentful of the people who *are* taking responsibility for their own growth and development.

Don't give your haters the microphone

When you begin to break out of society's mould, or you start to gradually peel off the label you've worn for so long, certain people will *always* have something to say about it—women in particular are notorious for this. They'll gossip, talk behind your back, make negative comments, be passive aggressive towards you, and sometimes even try and pull you down—but it's only because *they* feel weak or unconfident within themselves and wish they could do what you're doing. It's a very similar scenario to bullying—the bully is the one with the problem, not you, and they're taking their frustration out on you because that's easier than confronting their own issues.

When you're on a path to transform your life, you're instantly separating yourself from 99% of the population, which makes you stand out from the crowd. Whether you realise it or not, you're putting yourself out there, which makes you an easy target for haters and trolls.

Maybe you start losing a significant amount of weight and then certain people start commenting on how you look too thin or that you still look fat. Maybe you start recording videos of yourself singing and share them online and you get some cruel comments from an internet troll saying you sound terrible and not to quit your day job. Maybe you start blogging about fashion and someone tells you you've got no style. Whatever you decide to do, there will always be someone who has something bad to say—the sooner you learn take it on the chin, the better.

When I first started writing again, it only took a couple months before I began to write incredibly personal pieces about my feelings, my love life, and my deepest fears. I literally was pouring my heart and soul out onto the page and then putting it out there for the world to read. Sometimes only a few people would view it and there wouldn't be any comments; other times over a million people would read something and there would be a flood of people's thoughts and opinions on my words. I would say most of the time the comments were really positive, but the odd time someone would say something nasty with the intent of causing hurt. At first, it did affect me, but now I just let those insults roll off my back because I've realised that the moment you begin to let the negative opinions of others influence you or hold you back, you're signing over your power to *them*. You're letting them win.

As tempting as it may be to bite back, call people out on their hateful words, and get into petty arguments and slanging matches, all that does is give your haters a *voice*. Don't give them the microphone. Ignore it, rise above it, and don't look back for a second. Don't let anyone deter you from being *yourself*.

It's so easy to sit there and criticise others. People do this because it makes them feel better and more powerful than you in that moment. What they don't realise is that it's only fuelling them with negative energy and so that's all they end up receiving back from the universe. Hate only attracts more hate. It's easy to put others down, but it takes real courage to do what you're doing.

The best thing you can do when life gives you problems and pains is to turn them into something positive. So, when it comes to haters, I choose to use that negativity as *motivation*. Let people's judgements spur you on to succeed even more than yesterday. Let that drive you and be the reason why you work a little bit harder today, why you wake up a little bit earlier tomorrow morning, and why you push yourself further than you ever have done.

'To the doubters and naysayers and everyone who gave me hell and said I could not, that I would not or I must not—your resistance made me stronger, made me push harder, made me the fighter that I am today. It made me

the woman that I am today. So thank you."

— *Madonna*

Top tips to deal with negative comments

When it comes to the online world, specifically social media, if you don't want to completely remove yourself from it, that's more than okay. Personally, I *love* that complete strangers who have read my books are able to find me online and I'm then able to build a relationship with those women. It's difficult for me to explain just how moved and humble I feel upon hearing that my words have helped a woman through a painful time in her life, or inspired her to be more confident and happy with who she is. That's incredibly important to me, and I wouldn't want to cut myself off from that world.

What I would say is it's important not to base your worth on other people's opinions and comments—good or bad. It feels amazing when someone gives you a genuine compliment—I don't know a woman who *doesn't* want to be regularly told she's fabulous—but if you start falling into the trap of needing those positive comments in order to feel validated, then the negative ones will begin to have a much deeper impact on you too.

So by all means do your thing on social media, but don't place your value on what other people have to say, and only follow people who truly inspire you and cheer you on. Get comfortable deleting those negative nellies who do nothing but bitch and moan about their life along with everybody else's, and anyone else who doesn't make you instantly smile when you see their posts.

If you're a sensitive soul like me, you'll find it harder than most people to not take all words and actions as a personal stab to your heart. I remember when I got my first bad book review and it crushed me for a couple of days. Of course, even the world's best authors all have their fair share of bad reviews because not everyone is going to like what you have to say, and that's okay. But that's just *one* person's opinion. Why should you care what they think about you? Remember, if you try to please everyone, you'll only end up pleasing *nobody*. Do the best you can to develop a thick skin and just laugh things off. Be too busy working on your inner glow and chasing your own dreams to worry about what anybody else has to say.

Another great tip I've learned over the past few years is to simply ignore any abusive or negative comments you encounter along your journey. The truth is they aren't worth your time so don't lower yourself to someone else's crappy level. Keep your head held high *always*, and choose to rise above it. Glow getters don't deal in shade and bad vibes—we're all in on sunshine and smiles and using our energy to spread more love and peace in the world.

You determine your worth

Cast your mind back to when you were eight years old—young, innocent, and completely naive to the world. When they asked you who you were going to be, you'd tell them your wildest dreams without the slightest hesitation. You didn't care what anybody else thought, and anything and everything you wanted felt within reach. But that was before you began to face challenges and setbacks. Before other people got inside your head and started telling you what you could and couldn't do. Before that blind faith you were born with began to evaporate out of you.

Don't allow small minds or voices to hold you back from your destiny. The longer and harder you resist it, the more your world will begin to shake in protest and attempt to awake you to your calling. Don't be afraid to be *yourself,* for this is all you came here to do. This is who you're supposed to *be.*

This is *your* life. Make sure you live an extraordinary one. One you will look back on in years to come and swell with pride and love for the risks you took, how much you grew, and the way you fearlessly followed your heart no matter what.

Find a way back to the strength that used to live inside of that little girl. Find the courage to step up and do your heart's work. Find a way to the woman you know you're meant to be.

You are strong.
You are worthy.
You are capable.
You are fearless.
You are made of light.
You are made of *stars.*

GLOW

GUIDE

What's one hurtful thing someone has said to you that still plays on your mind?

Why does it hurt you?

Why do you value the opinion of the person who said it?

6 simple steps for dealing with haters

1. **Remember, it's really about *them*** - Behind anger, rests fear. When people attack you, it's usually because they themselves are afraid of something happening to them, or they're currently experiencing something difficult or painful in their own life. Be mindful of this the next time you receive a hurtful or negative comment.

2. **Don't take anything personally** - If you take what they're saying to heart, it means you think they might be right or you're agreeing with what they're saying. Don't take it personally—this will stop you from causing yourself even more pain.

3. **Take a step back** - Leave it for 24 hours—don't do anything, and it will go away. The moment you respond, the hate continues to spread and grow.

4. **You do you** - People will either love you, hate you, or won't care—so you should keep doing what you love and always do your best regardless of what anybody has to say about it. This is your life; you're not living it for anyone else.

5. **DELETE them (if you can)** - If it's a written comment, delete it where possible, and block any trolls. If it's someone in real life, don't engage with them and avoid them altogether if possible.

6. **Hate only fuels more hate** - When you get angry at someone else's actions or words, that anger rests inside you as negative energy which only harms you and can sometimes end up consuming you. It's easier said than done, but by only sending love and compassion to everyone, you're ending the cycle and turning negative vibes into something positive.

To download your free workbook that includes a full worksheet for this chapter's Glow Guide, along with the rest in this book, pop over to **shanijay.com/glowguide**.

FALL DOWN SEVEN TIMES,
STAND UP EIGHT

"The women whom I love and admire for their strength and grace did not get that way because shit worked out. They got that way because shit went wrong, and they handled it. They handled it in a thousand different ways on a thousand different days, but they handled it. Those women are my superheroes."

— Elizabeth Gilbert

I firmly believe that if something is easy to achieve we won't value it and it won't feel half as rewarding as when we push our way through something that truly tests us. Even the most fierce and fabulous women of this world have experienced failures on the road to greatness. You've gotta learn to take the sunshine with the storms, and this chapter is all about learning to do so.

You are not a robot—you're *human*

Why is it that every time we make the wrong choice, we beat ourselves up over it? We can't believe we did something so stupid, and we replay it over and over again in our minds, thinking if only we had acted differently...

It's as if we think we're robots or something, right?

Why did I do that?
I shouldn't have done that.
I should've know better.

And on and on and on, in toxic circles we go.

We've been *that* girl who has taken back a loser ex and believed their fake bullshit, only for them to screw us over again. We've been *that* girl who quit on something when it got too hard and we didn't believe we could succeed. We've been *that* girl who wasn't there for one of our closest friends when she needed us the most.

We make a mistake, cling on to it in our minds, and continue to punish ourselves for it over and over again. We do the same to other people in our lives by reminding them of the times they messed up and never truly letting it go. We forget that we're *human*. We all get things wrong, we all make poor decisions sometimes, and we all look back on certain days or events and wish we'd chosen differently.

By no means are we perfect, and I want you to realise that's *okay*. In fact, it's more than okay—it's frickin' awesome!! Perfection is a total snoozefest. It stifles creativity and attempts to mask our quirks and flaws—the very things that make us who we *are*.

With every mistake we make, we learn a valuable lesson. We grow, we become wiser, and hopefully we don't repeat the same mistakes again. The key is to make your mistakes—in fact, make plenty of them, but never allow your mistakes to make *you*.

So next time you have a blip and end up doing something you wish you could erase, remember that you are human. Don't be so hard on yourself. Cut yourself some slack now and again. Do what's in your power to make amends and carry on moving forwards. Take this as the growing experience it was meant as.

Learn the lesson and move onwards and upwards. The only way is *up*.

Failure is what happens when we're striving for something great

So many of us are scared of facing rejection or failure that we don't even try. We *don't* talk to that cute barista who serves us our coffee every day, we *don't* go for that promotion we desperately want at work, and we *don't* step outside of our comfort zones for just a moment so that we can have a shot at what it is our heart desires most.

If the fear of failure is stopping you from giving something a go, then listen up, sister—if you don't even *try*, there's a one hundred percent chance of you failing. The simple act of deciding to give something a go will automatically bring you one step closer to your goals and dreams than if you were to sit out on the sidelines and do nothing.

Don't allow those negative voices in the back of your head to bring you down before you've even started. If you're looking for one, you'll always find countless reasons why you can't do something, but you have to be strong enough to believe in all of the reasons why you *can* do it. At the end of the day, we're all just people with beating hearts and big dreams. There's no reason why someone you admire can succeed while you can't. There's no difference between you apart from the fact they never allowed failure to stand in the way of what they craved most.

Think about J.K. Rowling's incredible story. She separated from her husband, she ended up broke, depressed and living in a bedsit with her young child, and had pretty much hit rock bottom. But she loved to write so she continued to do so and she ended up writing the incredible story of Harry Potter which we have all come to know and love. Her manuscript got rejected from 12 different publishers, and she even got told to not quit her day job (imagine that!) before someone decided to say *yes*. She never gave up on herself and her dream of becoming a published author, and I'm incredibly thankful she didn't. It's a success story that gives us all *hope*.

As Rowling eloquently says:

> *"Failure taught me things about myself that I could have learned no other way. I discovered that I had a strong will, and more discipline than I had suspected. You might never fail on the scale I did, but some failure in life is inevitable. It is impossible to live without failing at something, unless you live so cautiously that you might as well not have lived at all—in which case, you fail by default."*

I remember hearing her speak those words a number of years ago, and they haven't left my heart since. As she quite rightly says, you can't navigate through this life without experiencing rejection and failures along the way, unless of course you don't *try* to accomplish anything. And if you don't try, you're simply wasting this beautiful gift of life you've been granted.

I think a lot of us fear making mistakes because we believe that those mistakes will damage us. Maybe in the past, our internal thoughts have allowed our mistakes to damage us in certain ways, or we've allowed others to make us feel worthless or inferior. We can be our own harshest critic, and we punish ourselves for not being perfect—which of course no one is.

Mistakes don't damage you; in fact, I've always believed they *cleanse* you. They help you to learn and to grow, to become wiser and stronger than you were yesterday. Look at them the right way, and they'll always turn you around and give you a little push in the direction you *should* be going.

When it comes to setbacks and failures, they are inevitable when you're striving for greatness. What matters most is how you choose to see them and then deal with them. If you view them in a negative light, they will infiltrate your mind and make you feel like a screw-up or worthless, but choose to see them as a growing experience and they will teach you a valuable lesson that helps you to move forward, ever closer to your higher self.

Always get back up

There will be times when you find yourself at rock bottom, feeling hopeless, worthless, second-guessing yourself, or wondering what the whole damn point of this *"changing my life"* thing is anyway. When you're putting yourself under so much internal pressure, coupled with any external pressure you're facing from other people, along with completely transforming your daily routine and thought processes, you're bound to sometimes feel like you've reached your absolute limits.

Trust me though you *haven't* and your possibilities are limitless. When you're on a mission to become the best woman you can be, things will inevitably go wrong along the way because that's *life*. You'll have setbacks and bad days, and some will be worse than others. You might find yourself bruised and crying on the floor, unsure of whether you can pick yourself back up again, but you must... because nobody else will.

It is only when you're at your worst that you will be able to discover your best. Without darkness, there is no light. Acknowledging our troubles and our pain, but learning to get back up and battle on through is where we discover our true strength. It's where we will discover who we have the potential to *become*. Life continues to test us because it's only when you're pushed to your limits that you can rise up stronger, wiser, and braver than you were before. There's a beautiful quote by Anais Nin that captures this sentiment:

> *"The flower that blooms in adversity is the most rare and beautiful of all."*

Realise you are stronger than anything life throws your way. Don't give up, keep paving your path forward, and it's only a matter of time before you'll look back and realise just how far you've travelled on your journey.

If you've lost the light and you find yourself unable to see, I want you to remember it is still there. Never stop believing it is there. When you find yourself seeking it out, remember that the light will always be shining wherever you may be. Sometimes, you'll just have to get moving and wander on a little further to be able to find it because the light resides within *you*. It always has and it always will.

You will be your own saviour. Don't let anything or anyone hold you down in this life or keep you from trying in the first place. You are not defined by your past or what has broken you. You are defined by how you *believe* and how you *rise* in spite of that pain.

Always remember, stars cannot shine without darkness. That very darkness is what makes them illuminate the depths of the night sky and come *alive*.

GLOW

GUIDE

#GLOWGETTERTRIBE

Take a moment to think of all the times you've made a mistake or failed at something.

What did you learn?

What can you improve on next time?

Learning to love your imperfections

As soon as you realise that perfection is an illusion, the easier you'll find it to move on from your mistakes and failures. None of us are perfect, and why would you want to be anyway? Perfection is boring!

Your mission today: Write yourself a letter of forgiveness.

Today is the day you stop allowing your mistakes to make you.

Forgive yourself in this letter for all of the mistakes, setbacks, and failures you continue to carry around with you. Let any guilt or suffering pour out of you as you put pen to paper. Now, burn the letter, or rip it up into shreds. Let this signify that those mistakes are in your past and don't belong here in the future you're creating.

Focus on how you can better learn to deal with mistakes and failures from today. The very next time you mess up (however big or small it might seem), remind yourself that you are only human, and look at this as an opportunity to grow and become wiser. And don't forget to thank the universe for this valuable lesson!

Download your free workbook at **shanijay.com/glowguide**, which contains all the detailed worksheets that go along with every Glow Guide in this book, plus so much more!

Dear...

RAISE THE BAR

"There is no limit to what we, as women, can accomplish."

— Michelle Obama

What you've gotta remember about this journey is it doesn't have a final destination—and it's not supposed to either. Transformation and growth are on-going. Once you reach your end goal, you should always find a slightly bigger one to replace it with to ensure you keep challenging yourself and discovering what you're truly capable of when you put your whole heart into something.

This is simply the beginning for you.

How to stay on track and not slip into old habits

I'd be breaking girl code if I told you it's going to be easy staying on track all the time and that you won't have bad days because the reality is you *will*—all of us do. All it takes is something small to trigger a switch within us that sends us spiralling back into our old habits, sometimes without us even noticing it, until a few weeks or months later when we stop and realise we've completely relapsed.

Remember, if you have a setback that's *okay*. Acknowledge that it happened and try to figure out what the root cause was so that you can be aware if it crops up again in the future. Always look at tomorrow as a fresh start, and begin each new day with a positive mind, without carting around the baggage of your yesterdays. Just because things got a little out of control today or you didn't quite stick to your plan, it doesn't mean you've failed or that you should give up. Life is going to throw so many things your way; it's up to you to decide whether you're going to let them knock you out or whether you're going to get back up again and push forward.

Think about all that you *have* achieved so far, all of the sacrifices you've made, and why you embarked on this mission in the first place. Get yourself back on track and keep going. As long as you always do your best, that's all that matters.

The TWO things you must do when you reach your goal

I think so many of us forget to pause after achieving something we've worked incredibly hard for, and just dive headfirst into the next thing we want. It's great to be motivated like that and to keep on striving for more, and it might be the most productive approach to keep going while you're on a good run, but this is a recipe for burnout. We all need that precious time to stop and reflect, check in with ourselves, and make sure we're heading the right way.

I remember when my first book was published, and while I was extremely proud and overwhelmed in that moment, I didn't really allow it to be more than just a moment. I didn't stop to celebrate, and I was already in the middle of writing my *next* book. Instead of feeling accomplished, I was allowing myself to get caught up in the stress and gravity of the new task I'd taken on. If I could go back, I'd throw myself a fabulous party with confetti-filled balloons, find a small-ish commemorative gift to give to myself to mark the special occasion, eat decadent chocolate cake and strawberries, and drink pretty pink champagne!

So when you reach your first BIG goal, the first thing to do, before you do *anything* else, is to CELEBRATE, SISTER! Allow yourself the pleasure of looking back in awe at how far you've come, how you've managed to drastically turn your life around, and the many steps you've taken towards the woman you've always dreamed of being since you were a little girl. Even when it seems small or insignificant, because that's what will keep pushing you forward and comfort you when nothing seems to be going your way. Don't brush any of your achievements off as "small"—each and every one of them play a role in your journey.

What you may not realise yet is all of those small steps add up, and before you know it, you'll stop and take a look at your life and be absolutely amazed at just how far you've come. A victory, no matter how small, is still success. You're moving in the right direction, slowly but surely. Don't ever feel stupid or afraid to be proud of something you have achieved. Stand up, stand tall, and ALWAYS celebrate. Because who cares if no one's cheering with you? You deserve to feel all kinds of *amazing*, every single day of your life. Strong, accomplished, worthy, fabulous, and unstoppable. Cheers to that!

The second important task whenever you meet a goal is to set a *new* one. Now you *might* think that's a recipe for never being content with your current circumstances and what you've achieved, but that's not the case. Wherever you may be on your transformation journey right now, I've found it's imperative to keep your levels of motivation and inspiration up, even after you've reached your initial goals. Continually raising the bar a little higher helps you to do this. By all means, celebrate every single one of your victories, but keep on challenging yourself past those wins because this is how you'll continue to grow and be better with each new day.

Every time I reach one of my goals, I replace it with a slightly bigger one to ensure I'm pushing myself and dangling something that's shiny and exciting enough in front of me that I want to keep getting up each day and throw everything I've got into it. Start small, but don't be afraid to climb higher and higher in pursuit of your grandest, wildest dream. If you can dream it, you can live it, and you've now got the handy success secrets to know *exactly* how to do it!

Supporting other women on their journey

I'm a firm believer in karma—when we commit to loving and supporting others, life in turn will love and support us in wondrous ways.

Think back to how you felt before you decided to change your life or when you first began your journey. You might've been a mix of anxious, scared, or stressed. You might've had no idea how or where to begin. Think about the kind of support you were lucky enough to receive along the way, or if you weren't fortunate enough to have any, think about the kind of support you would have greatly benefitted from and been thankful for. The kind that would have made your journey a little easier or more comfortable.

Now go and *be* that support for another glow getter. Reach out, be helpful and supportive within your real life friendships and acquaintance circle, as well as your online networks too. It doesn't have to take up much of your time—even the smallest gesture like sending someone a message filled with words of encouragement, telling them you're there for them if they ever need advice, or giving them that little push we all need to get started can really make a difference in someone's journey. Encourage other women with their own transformations because sometimes all we need is to know that someone *believes* in us, in order to finally start believing in ourselves. Always strive to be the woman you wish was there for you during your darkest days when you were struggling alone.

Once you're done reading this book, share it with a woman in your world who could really benefit from it, or gift them the first two chapters for free by sending them to **shanijay.com/free**.

Spreading the love will not only create joy in other's lives, but it will also help you to stay focused and motivated on your own journey because you've gotta practice what you preach, glow getter! You never know who you're inspiring, who's looking up to you, or whose rainy day you're lighting up with sparkling sunshine, love, and light when they're trapped in darkness. Someone might just end up turning their life around because *you* helped them see it's not only possible, but proven—because you've lived it.

The wonderful thing about this life is that we can always look inside ourselves and give just a little bit more today than we did yesterday. We have no real limits, only those we place on ourselves. As you wake up each morning, ask yourself, who do you want to be? What will your story be? Are you aligning your day with the wishes of your heart and your soul? This is how you'll get your *glow*, inside and out.

GLOW

GUIDE

How does it feel to have succeeded in sticking to and reaching your goal?

What do you know now that you didn't know before you set out on this journey?

How has this achievement contributed to becoming the woman you want to be and designing the life you want to live?

Tips for CELEBRATING like you mean it!

I've put together a few fun ideas of what you can do to mark the occasion of finally reaching one of your goals and congratulate yourself like you truly mean it (I hope you do!):

- ♥ Pop a bottle of pink bubbly (or your drink of choice) and toast to your fabulousness!
- ♥ Dine at a restaurant that has been on your to-visit list forever.
- ♥ Treat yourself to a small gift to mark the occasion (it doesn't have to be anything expensive!).
- ♥ Spend an entire day doing whatever you want to do, and don't feel guilty for a second.
- ♥ Bake yourself one of those fancy rainbow-layered unicorn cakes, invite your besties over to share it with you, and devour as much of it as you wish!
- ♥ Book a fancy massage or retreat to unwind from any stress or tension that has built up in the process.
- ♥ Call your best friend and tell her how amazing you are (you ARE!).
- ♥ Buy a confetti gun and sprinkle that rainbow like you mean it!
- ♥ Write a list of everything you learned from this experience.
- ♥ Put on your favourite song and just DANCE.
- ♥ Text/email/call all your loved ones to tell them the good news, so they can shower you with compliments (and maybe gifts too).

- Write down what you've achieved, and pin it up somewhere you'll see it every day and be reminded of how far you've come.
- Stock up on all your favourite snacks, sit back, and watch your favourite movie.
- Write a handwritten letter (using your prettiest stationery) of gratitude to someone who helped you on your journey.
- Take a day off from work (no explanation needed).
- Throw a party (this is a great one for those BIG goals!).
- Take a selfie so you can remember yourself on this fabulous day in years to come.
- Spread the love, reach out to a fellow glow getter, and give her the best piece of advice you'd give your old self today.

Now it's time to raise the bar: What will your next goal be?

Think BIGGER than you did last time, and make sure it excites you enough to keep on working for it!

You can also head to **shanijay.com/glowguide** and download your free workbook that includes plenty more tips and a full worksheet for this chapter's Glow Guide, along with all the rest in this book!

"Something will grow from all that you're going through.

And it will be you."

— Anon.

A FINAL WORD:
YOU'VE GOT THIS

This life will be what you choose to make of it, and it comes and goes in a flash. At the end of your time here, you want to be able to look back and know that every single day you spent on this earth was one filled with love, light, and your heartsong. You want to know that you did everything in your power to be the *best* woman you could possibly be. You want to be able to say you *chose* your life; you didn't simply settle for the path of least resistance.

My wish is that you've reached the end of this book feeling inspired and determined to commit to transforming your life and reassured that no matter what may come your way you can handle it because you're now a fearless and fabulous glow getter. This journey, though not easy, will be the most rewarding of all.

If you carry just one message with you from this book, let it be those three vital elements outlined at the very beginning: *vision*, *promise*, and *energy*. Know what you want, promise to show up for yourself daily, and be prepared to put in the hard work. These three elements form the foundation of a true commitment and will be the forces that guide and spur you on through anything.

This book will remain here for you to re-visit anytime you experience one of these setbacks or challenges, and anytime you need to seek clarity and a path to guide you forward. Anytime you decide to embark on a new goal or pivot your life a new direction, you can look back to chapter one and start all over again.

Even if you're only just beginning to make some bold changes in your life, I want you to know I believe in you, glow getter. I believe in your gift, your heart, and the message you are carrying. I believe the world needs you and your magic in it. You can do this. This is your *destiny*.

I hope you find what you're looking for. I hope you find your way to what your heart and soul crave most. I hope you learn to look in the mirror and be proud of the beautiful woman staring back at you, regardless of where you are on your journey, or how far you have left to go. I hope you find *yourself* somewhere along the way too.

Get on out there, turn those can'ts into *cans*, and those beautiful dreams into *plans*.

Thank you for reading, beautiful!

I couldn't do what I do without my readers, so thank you from the bottom of my heart for choosing this book.

Did you enjoy *Glow Getter*?

If the answer is YES, it would mean so much if you could take two minutes of your time right now to leave a short review on Amazon.

This helps other women to find the book and spread the love!

I read every single one of your comments and I'm so thankful for them all.

Snap a selfie!

I LOVE seeing where in the world my books have travelled to, so if you're on Instagram, snap a selfie of yourself with your copy of *Glow Getter*, and tag me @shanijaywriter
#GLOWGETTERTRIBE

ACKNOWLEDGMENTS

A book always goes far beyond its author, and this one is no exception. Without the following special souls, this book wouldn't have made it into your hands.

Thank you to my wonderful family for all their love and support over the years—I don't say it enough, but I love you and can't thank you enough for everything you've done for me.

To Sam—I feel incredibly lucky to have found someone who understands and supports me the way that you do. You mean more to me than you'll ever know.

Thank you to my brilliant editor, Caitlin—you always know how to make my words sparkle a little brighter.

A special shout-out to the soul sisters on my launch team—thank you for cheering me on, spreading the love, and being your awesome selves.

And a final thank you to *you,* beautiful lady, for choosing this book and for reading all the way to here.

ABOUT SHANI

Shani is a bestselling author, content creation business owner, life coach, and self-love advocate. She loves exploring and working from new parts of the world, the sight of gorgeous fresh flowers on her desk every day while she writes, and all things pink and glittery.

In 2016, Shani founded The Glow Getter Tribe—a self-love and kindness movement which helps young girls and women worldwide feel happy, confident, and beautiful starting from the inside out. She is the author of *Bloom, The Babe Bible,* and *Glow Getter.* And her writing has been featured on many internationally recognised platforms including *The Huffington Post, Teen Vogue,* and *Thought Catalog.*

Shani believes in kindness, karma, true love, never giving up until you create a dream world you're crazy in love with, and that words truly do have the power to transform your life.

Shani would like nothing more than to get to know you better! If you're interested in finding out more about Shani and joining her mission, head to shanijay.com to learn more.

Connect with Shani:

- ♥ Visit my website and blog: shanijay.com
- ♥ Instagram: @shanijaywriter
- ♥ Facebook: Shani Jay Writer
- ♥ Check out my other books: *Bloom,* and *The Babe Bible,* on Amazon.

All the Glow Guides from this book, extra worksheets, printouts and bonuses can be found at: **shanijay.com/glowguide**

See you soon,
glow getter.

Made in the USA
Coppell, TX
17 September 2020